Architecture, Industry and Innovation   The Early Work of Nicholas Grimshaw & Partners

Architecture, Industry and Innovation   The Early Work of Nicholas Grimshaw & Partners

Colin Amery

Phaidon Press Limited
Regent's Wharf
All Saints Street
London N1 9PA

First published 1995

© 1995 Phaidon Press Limited

Frontispiece
Nick Grimshaw explains his
concept for the Service Tower
to Richard Buckminster Fuller
in 1968

ISBN 0 7148 2923 4

A CIP catalogue record for
this book is available from the
British Library

Printed in Hong Kong

Photographic credits

Ove Arup and Partners: p153; Clive Boursnell: p193 (bottom); Crispin Boyle Photography: p186 (bottom); Richard Bryant / Arcaid: p56 (left); Hanya Chlala: p159; John Donat: pp76 (top left), 80 (top and bottom), 81, 84 (top and bottom); Michael Dyer Associates: pp41, 44 (top), 76 (centre and bottom), 78, 139, 152; Eames Office: p13; Don Gray: pp131, 132, 133, 134, 135 (top and left); Lavinia Grimshaw: p237 (top); Nicholas Grimshaw & Partners: pp8, 39 (centre), 42 (top), 46, 47 (top, centre and bottom), 48 (top), 75, 83 (top and bottom), 163, 181, 198, 214; Nick Grimshaw: pp35 (right), 42 (bottom), 186 (top); Alistair Hunter: pp154, 158; Ken Kirkwood: pp93, 97, 98, 99, 100, 101; Jo Reid and John Peck: pp14, 15, 61, 62 (top and left), 63, 64, 65 (top), 77, 82, 85, 89, 90–91, 105, 106, 108, 109, 113, 114, 117, 118, 119, 123, 124, 125, 126, 127, 140–41, 142 (top), 143, 144, 145, 146, 147, 151, 155, 165, 166–67, 171, 172, 173, 174, 175, 176, 177, 182–83, 184, 185, 187, 192, 194, 195, 196, 197, 199, 200, 201, 205, 206, 207, 208, 209, 213, 215, 216, 217, 219, 220, 221, 225, 226, 227, 228, 229, 230, 232, 233, 234, 235, 236, 237 (bottom), 239, 240–41; Jeff Scherer: pp69, 70 (top left and right, and bottom), 71, 79 (top); Tim Street Porter: pp35 (left), 57; Hin Tan: p191; Tessa Traeger: pp2, 45, 49, 53, 55 (top and bottom); Andrew Whalley: p37 (centre).

Note

The projects described on pages 40 to 121 were carried out by Nick Grimshaw during the time he was a partner in the practice entitled Farrell / Grimshaw Partnership.

Service Tower, Student
Hostel, London, 1967.

8

Introduction   Colin Amery

In my library, books about Nicholas Grimshaw lie between books on Eileen Gray and Hector Guimard. Not such a bad place to be filed and, in a way, rather appropriate. Eileen Gray lived and worked in Paris for 70 years and died aged 98 in 1976. She was one of the few British architects of this century who was a creative modernist. She was unusual in wanting to work as a European and, like Grimshaw, had a rare understanding of the importance of design as an all-embracing and difficult discipline. She had an almost secret influence on the century – unlike architects today she shunned publicity; perhaps as a result, she completed very few major projects. Despite this, much of the essence of her thought processes and design skills can be seen in microcosm in her furniture and even her carpet designs.

Hector Guimard (1867–1942) was in some ways much less of a rationalist, but he had a brilliant feel for materials. He worked with metal, glass and faience, most notably on his masterpiece, the Castel Berenger in Paris. Like Grimshaw, he understood the potential of new architectural materials and developed them into a language and style that was highly individual. He was fortunate in his clients who allowed him to develop the more extreme elements of French Art Nouveau, particularly on the Paris Métro.

This fortuitous placing of Grimshaw on the library shelf may not put him exactly where he would like to be in terms of his place in architectural history, but it does offer him two appropriate godparents. Indeed it is too soon, when an architect is at the height of his powers and clearly developing and changing, to place him in history at all. This essay introduces a volume that deals with his work only from 1967 to 1988, and so it is not the place to reach any final judgement about his complete career.

In 1988, when I wrote the introductory essay for the catalogue of the major Royal Institute of British Architects exhibition on Grimshaw's work, 'Product and Process', there was a sense that Grimshaw and the world were anticipating a change of scale in his output. That has now happened with tremendous panache and bravery, and these projects are covered in detail in *Structure, Space and Skin* which examines his architecture from the period 1988–93. Key among this body of work are the British Pavilion at Expo 92 in Seville, the Waterloo Channel Tunnel Railway Terminal in London, the Berlin Stock Exchange and Communications Centre, the headquarters of the Royal Automobile Club, as well as the competition entries for Heathrow Airport and the Lisbon Railway Station.

This volume, however, looks at the developing roots of Grimshaw's architecture and, by the time it reaches the key commission of the Financial Times Printing Works, all the evidence is there of the future large-scale flowering. Alongside his British peers, Sir Norman Foster and Sir Richard Rogers, Grimshaw may be seen as having gradually covered a slightly wider and more innovative landscape. He is the youngest of the trio by several years and he has made haste steadily without the fanfare of too much publicity or the taking on of the role of propagandist. He has always been steady, building up a loyal team of largely young people and remaining personally reticent, letting the buildings speak for themselves.

But where do his buildings belong in the pluralistic world of late-20th century architecture? First of all it is important to look at the architect's own roots.

It is not unimportant to recall that Grimshaw almost became an engineer. His father was an aircraft engineer and his great-grandfather was a pioneering civil engineer who built dams and bridges on the River Nile in Egypt. Atkinson Grimshaw was another ancestor – he was a well-known Victorian painter, famous for his extraordinary concern for precise detail in his paintings, as well as his almost uncanny ability to paint night and moonlit scenes. If there is a genetic basis for talent, the Grimshaw gene seems to contain traits that encouraged Nicholas Grimshaw to follow on his inherited interest in engineering and love of detail. There is also an underlying art in his architecture that has taken time to emerge.

After leaving the College of Art in Edinburgh, he was to spend three years in the architectural hothouse of the 1960s, the Architectural Association in London. Here he was tutored by Cedric Price and John Winter. Inevitably he came under the influence of Peter Cook and the Archigram crowd who were (then as now) promoting a fantasy world of technological imagery that created a powerful, but mainly graphic effect. The 1960s were strange and exciting times. There was a belief that technology could not only improve the efficiency of the world, but also somehow transform it morally for the better.

In Britain, the early appreciation of a promising technological future had begun with the Festival of Britain in 1951. In many ways it was a built version of a rather innocent view of the future based upon the certainties of scientific discovery. It promoted a sense of excitement that inspired students and led some into the exploration of space and nuclear physics, and even architecture. Nick Grimshaw can recall his early enthusiasm for the Dome of Discovery and interest in the Skylon, an early tensile structure by Powell and Moya; this was the Tatlin Tower of its day, a technically clever form with no precise symbolic meaning.

The Festival evoked the emergence of a future that did not lose sight of its Victorian source in the great British exhibition. In many ways, it was the revival of interest in things Victorian, especially the railway termini and the Crystal Palace, that made perceptive architects look again at Sir Joseph Paxton's genius. Paxton has always been a clear influence upon those British architects who explored steel and glass technology. Grimshaw himself describes the Crystal Palace as one of the most significant buildings of the last two centuries. In the Lord Reilly memorial lecture given in October 1992, Grimshaw expressed his admiration for the building; he saw it as an example of an entirely well-considered construction. He rightly appreciated the skill and care that went into the process of prefabrication, and the installation of these components from specially-designed travelling gantries, where every dimension had to be coordinated with intense care.

I imagine that another aspect of Paxton's work admired by Grimshaw is his progress from the initial concept to the final building. From the earliest stages, the sketch concepts for the Great Exhibition building had a very clear image of a central nave buttressed by

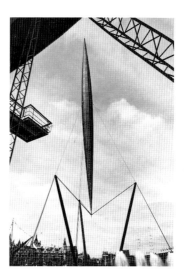

Skylon, Festival of Britain, by Powell and Moya, London, 1951.

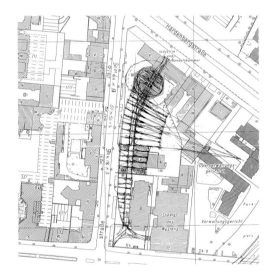

Berlin Stock Exchange and
Communications Centre,
1991–95, concept sketch
by Nick Grimshaw.

aisles. It was undoubtedly this clarity of concept that
made possible its development in such a consistent,
detailed and thorough way. This is very much how
Grimshaw works. His concept sketches for the Berlin
Stock Exchange, for example, or the more modest
Homebase store in West London, have in them the
complete essence of the final design. This is not shown
in any skeletal way, but as a solid, clear yet preliminary
vision of the final three-dimensional solution.

In architecture, the excitement of the Festival of
Britain site found support and a propaganda base at the
Architectural Review, which saw a future for this
picturesque kind of architectural townscape for newly-
planned towns and cities in the UK. The more
experimental and international architectural concerns to
appear at the Festival, and develop as the post-war years
led to a more prosperous and conjectural period, were
published in the pages of *Architectural Design* – an
influential bible among students at the time. At that
time, there were also the writings of the late Reyner
Banham – his *Theory and Design in the First Machine
Age*, published in 1960, was a palpable symbol of the
excitement of a new machine age. Banham interpreted
the work of the American theorist and futurist
Buckminster Fuller for the first time, offering both a
criticism and an analysis of the International Modern
style which revealed its strengths as well as its technical
weaknesses.

Buckminster Fuller and the writer, Marshall McLuhan,
were the two Americans who were seized upon as
prophets and missionaries for the second half of the
20th century. The gospel according to McLuhan was
that the world would soon have an infinite technical

capacity to communicate by computer, telephone line
and satellite. Ideas would flash around the world, but
exactly what the communicated message would be was
uncertain. The medium became the message – it was an
approach that was to apply even to architecture and the
development of architectural ideas.

At the Architectural Association, many of the regular
tutors were British pioneers of modernism, passing on
the flame to the next generation. Among them was
Maxwell Fry and his wife Jane Drew, who had worked
with Le Corbusier in India. It was Fry who examined the
young Grimshaw's thesis on the use of the grid in the
planning of Greek towns and fired a warning shot to the
student that his approach was 'mechanistic at the
expense of architectural factors'. This was a lesson soon
absorbed and never forgotten by Grimshaw. In many
ways it is the key to much of his thinking about
architecture today – an awareness of the value of the
structural and mechanical, but combined with an
understanding of the art of architecture.

There were other forces at work at the time besides
the influential excitement of the Architectural
Association and the climate of optimism about the
machine age. There was a strong sense of the *Zeitgeist*
of the 1960s that acted as a guiding force for the
creative spirits of the time. Some of the architects
trained in that period have never lost the conviction
that architecture reflects the moral imperative of the
time and expresses the spirit of the age. Grimshaw
would not deny this, but his work and his approach is
perhaps more genuinely rational. Architecture for him is
about the solving of pragmatic and technical problems
in a steady, careful and practical way. Out of this direct

approach comes an architecture which is mistakenly seen as 'high-tech' but is, in fact, well-tempered functional engineering married to the fundamental principles of architecture. It is an architecture whose roots can be traced from the Iron Bridge in 1776 through the work of Paxton and Brunel to Owen Williams. It shares the engineering base of much of the best 20th century British architecture.

Grimshaw's later work is also more experimental and inventive than that of some of his colleagues who work in a similar vein. But this flexibility is a relatively recent development, and the way it has happened is revealing of the character of the man. For many years Grimshaw was seen as an architect who, like Foster, had found that industrial sheds and enclosures provided a better background for an experimental architecture than any other field. The scope for such innovation grew with the advent of the business park and the expanding towns of the 1970s. Alongside these early sheds were the more individual and developed designs, like Herman Miller in Bath and the Ice Rink in Oxford; but once these were perfected they were often refined and repeated. It is clear in the pages that follow that Grimshaw believes in very gradual but real progress in design. Very few elements of his work are untested, and familiar well-tried ones are repeated in an almost fugue-like way. Arrangements of the parts produce subtly different sets of variations, rather like a series of originals.

What Grimshaw's early work clearly shows is that he is an architect who defines a programme in component terms. This is not as easy as it looks because it demands a special kind of selective mind; a method of planning and designing that refines a palette of components in

a rigorous way. When he looked at the Crystal Palace, Grimshaw measured its success in terms of the three elemental criteria that govern his own work, 'structure, space and skin'. If these three areas create the architecture, it is the selection and design of the individual components that determine a building's functionality.

Grimshaw argues that when he uses elements like glass panels, steel beams and castings he is working in the same way that architects have always used bricks, stone and timber. Indeed he has often questioned the definition of 'traditional materials'. He points out that, after all, glass has been in use for at least 3,000 years, and even steel goes back a few centuries. Some of his contemporaries, like Sir Michael Hopkins and Renzo Piano, have built major buildings in a wide range of traditional materials. But, to date, Grimshaw has not had the opportunity, although his own country home in Norfolk has had the benefit of his skills applied to a stone building.

Grimshaw maintains that in his use of glass, aluminium and steel he is, in fact, only carrying on the mainstream of British architecture. He believes that good construction – the careful putting together of things – has always been the basis of building in this country. From timber-framed houses in Elizabethan times to today's steel and glass masterpieces, careful detailing has always been the key to all good architects' work.

He believes passionately that materials and the details that are created with them are the foundations of the architect's art – just like the palette of a painter. He dismisses much of the architecture of the 1980s,

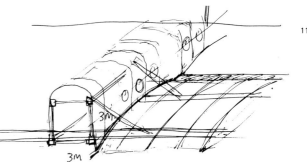

11

Homebase Store, Brentford, 1987, concept sketch by Nick Grimshaw.

Component housing system,
1951 by Jean Prouvé.

which sought to ape the past in a shallow visual way, terming it 'wallpaper architecture'. He believes that the architects of these buildings have shown so little understanding of construction and materials that their creations have no lasting quality.

Grimshaw is probably right in his emphasis on materials as the root of good modern architecture. One could cite Le Corbusier's mastery of concrete, Aalto's brilliance with brick and timber construction and, of course, Mies van der Rohe's sublime details in steel and bronze. However, there are two people who have equal significance for Grimshaw, not only because of their attitude to the exploration of modern materials and technology, but also because of their philosophy; these two people are Jean Prouvé and Charles Eames.

Prouvé was born in 1901. He was not an architect – he trained as an iron-worker and blacksmith – but he spent most of his life trying to move the building industry and architects out of the Middle Ages. In fact he did not approve of the architectural profession, he felt that the separation of architect and designer was the principal cause of low standards of modern design and construction. He wrote an illuminating article in 1970 that could as easily apply to the 1990s and the whole question of the state of the art of architecture:

Where have we got to? Certainly there is an architecture being built that we call 'modern', let's say it is contemporary. Most of us are agreed that it does not, on the whole, provoke the same architectural experience as that felt by people in front of the great architectural ensembles of the past; that is undeniable.

Would the reason not be a lack of courage in the use of the new materials that mechanization has put at our disposal? Is there not, too, a deficiency of architectural inspiration in relation to these means?

Prouvé was worried about the cult of personality among architects, feeling that it undermined the efforts of the manufacturers to standardize a kit of workable parts:

We note that the old and admired architectural entities were often very uniform. That's a troubling thought. Industrialists are confused because, for the 'personalities' of architecture, they are obliged to study and adapt continuously. The Master Builders, who are tempted to evolve, often make industrialists suffer by their personal demands – demands that are often inappropriate to the materials chosen. Such tasks are superhuman and cruel to both men and tools. Prices, too, are very high. And it happens that certain clever artisans, capable of improvisation, compete with the industrialists.

Prouvé understood and explained clearly the problems of industrializing buildings, and he and Grimshaw see the problem of the architect's ego obstructing, instead of advancing, the process of industrialization. One of the blessings of any recession is that all architects have to understand the importance of building economy.

Prouvé's particular love, and one that is shared by Grimshaw, was for thin sheets of metal cladding that are ridged or crimped to give them added strength. In the Roland Garros Flying Club, which he built in the 1930s with the architects Beaudouin and Lods, walls, floors, roof and ramp were all constructed from machine-made pressed metal. He went on into the 1960s making finely detailed industrialized houses and units for industry, working out every element of the buildings as though no one had built a building before. His work demonstrates that there is a new building process and that it needs architects to become closely involved in industry for it to make real progress. Grimshaw is a true disciple, fascinated by the method and, as the majority of buildings selected for this volume show, modest enough to let the industrial process play a major part in the design. He has taken on Prouvé's mantle, and wears it with appropriate modesty.

Charles Eames' work has been another important influence. Grimshaw claims to see a great democracy in Eames' designs, something that he aims for in his own architecture. Charles Eames, with his wife and partner Ray, invented a complete and all-inclusive world of design. They saw beauty in the commonplace and really began a radically new way of looking at the world. They were not concerned with high art, but with the look of the everyday commercial world, freely combining 'designed' objects with the 'found'. They amassed a glorious and colourful collection of pieces in the house they designed for themselves in Pacific Palisades in Los Angeles (1949). The house itself is a classic 'kit of parts'; it was built from windows and panels that came straight from trade catalogues and were fixed directly onto the steel frame. The attitude of the designers and the atmosphere of their house was an inspiration to many architects. Their conviction that it is possible to make a better and more beautiful world from the everyday things around them heartened architects like Grimshaw

and continues to influence them in their work.

I remember being entertained to tea by Ray Eames when I went to see their house; it was a bright warm Californian day, but she lit vivid pink candles on the tables to make the setting more welcoming and festive. In fact the whole meal was pink, with rose-coloured cake and bowls of fresh strawberries. She demonstrated in her life and her collections that the modern style need not be colourless and empty, but can be sensual and even luxurious.

There is a strong element of pure pleasure about good design, something that can be seen and enjoyed in the Grimshaw office and in many of the buildings in this book. There is also the sense of the pleasure in sheer constructional ingenuity, something very present in the Eames House and in the office of Nicholas Grimshaw. The delight in models, the amazement at the ingenuity of skeletons, the patent pleasure in a well-made object, whether it is a car radio or a rocket. This simple pleasure and enthusiasm infuses Grimshaw's work, in the making of the parts and the creation of the whole.

Thomas Aquinas provided us with a good definition of aesthetics – it must involve the search for three things: clarity, integrity and proportion. They are good elements to define any serious piece of architecture. In the search for clarity in Grimshaw's work this can be seen to arise from the earliest discussions with the client: clarity of intention produces clarity of architecture. Integrity is the same thing as honesty; it is not hard to find in the work of this practice because the designers are like terriers worrying away at the detail, at the materials, at the quality of everything, especially

Eames House by Charles and Ray Eames, Pacific Palisades, California 1949, here seen in construction.

Superstore for Sainsbury's,
Camden, London, 1986–88

when commercial budgets are tight. Proportion is to do with balance, symmetry and perspective. These have to relate harmoniously to each other if it is architecture rather than just building that you are looking for. To achieve this ten times out of ten is difficult, but in Grimshaw's work it clearly underlies everything.

As his approach has refined and evolved, the buildings of the early 1990s have brought a new dimension of meaning to Grimshaw's architecture. It is possible for the early projects to be seen with new eyes in the light of the latest work. In fact distance does two things, it enables us to see some of the roots of the most recent buildings – but it also reveals, through the architect's creative development, some aspects of the way he works.

The Sussex Gardens Service Tower, the first building illustrated in this book, gives several insights. Firstly, it is a humane concept: an almost joyous provision of sanitary facilities in a single mixed-use tower which avoided the traditional concept of isolated corridor bathrooms. This project (which, it must be remembered, was Grimshaw's first after leaving the AA) already showed an extraordinary mastery of detail. Its helical form also illustrated Grimshaw's great interest in geometry. (Purely coincidentally, this was the time of Crick and Watson's discovery of the structure of DNA based on the double helix.)

The block of flats at Park Road demonstrated Grimshaw's developing interest in 'technology transfer'. At the time Ronan Point was being built in heavy pre-cast concrete, he was suggesting that lightweight materials, such as aluminium backed up by fibreglass insulation, could do the job just as well.

With the Citroën Warehouse, Grimshaw demonstrated a sensitivity to landscape later seen at the Furniture Factory for Vitra and the Oxford Ice Rink, where he clearly showed that 20th century building technology could be used in a way that was sympathetic to its surroundings. His profound belief that people should be able to manipulate their surroundings was developed in the buildings for Editions Van de Velde, Herman Miller, and at Winwick Quay. Here, by using carefully detailed cladding systems, he demonstrated that a simple industrial building could take on the evolving character of a shell capable of being altered to suit the changing needs of users and the processes inside.

The enormous force that the clear expression of structure can give to a building is first seen at the Sports Hall for IBM, where the structure seems to echo the branches of the surrounding trees. This technique is developed to achieve a bravura performance at the Oxford Ice Rink where the tension structure somehow signals the thrill and excitement of the activity inside.

Then at the Financial Times Printing Works, a building with a more formal and disciplined approach, support for the facade, for the roof and for the cleaning gantries are all combined in one clear system. This apparently simple move allows the all-glass facade and the revelation of the printing activity within.

Finally, with the supermarket project for Sainsbury's in Camden Town, one can see Grimshaw coming to terms with urban quality. Scale, grain and colour have been well considered here and point the way to the successful urbanity manifested in his current buildings at Waterloo Station in London and for the Stock Exchange in Berlin.

What might be thought of as the primary works in this volume should perhaps be seen as the foundation stones for the more major works. They all, however small, follow certain truths: the flexible plan, an expressed structure, a difference between the served and the servant spaces, and the visible and increasingly expressive celebration of machine-made componentry.

I am intrigued by Grimshaw's marriage of functionalist and expressionist ideas. I suspect that the Stock Exchange in Berlin will be the best building yet because it will be both a technical wonder and an organic part of the city. It has more character than its surroundings and its nature is almost anthropomorphic and visceral, like a creature that has settled in the city from elsewhere.

In terms of architectural history, I sense that there is a change in the air that is as profound as the end of medieval architecture and the arrival of the Renaissance and the printing press. Churches were once read like books; they told the story of religion directly and visually to populations that could not read. As superstition was replaced by reason in architecture, religion is replaced by secular aestheticism.

If we accept, as the history of art has demonstrated, that the development of the imagination precedes the development of reason, then the work of this particular architect in the 1990s shows an imagination moving into a more expressive mode. He uses the materials available to him to articulate the extraordinary technological changes in the late-20th century. However, it is easier for painters to imagine and make visible the effects of the microchip than it is for an architect to design an expensive and complex building that expresses the ideas behind the current technology. There are signs everywhere that the thrall of technology is loosening to release a more expressive spirit which has the potential to extend our knowledge of contemporary reality.

Grimshaw rightly believes that his buildings have improved the quality of life in the working world. His career, as this book clearly demonstrates, has proceeded gradually, ensuring along the way that the problems of structure, flexibility, materials, energy efficiency and imagery are tackled progressively in each new project. In his office a new design develops carefully, step by step, with infinite discussion among the whole team. Care is the key to the nature of his work. Endless care to see that every detail is correct – but it is care that provides the secure base for flights of the architectural imagination.

Financial Times Printing Works, London Docklands, 1987–88.

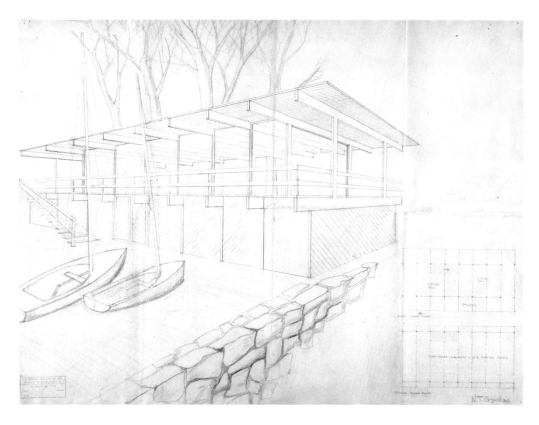

One of Nick Grimshaw's first
year projects at Edinburgh Art
College in 1960: a sailing club
drawn in pencil on handmade
paper.

Autobiographical note   Nick Grimshaw

As I write this note, trains have just started running to
Paris from the International Terminal at Waterloo, the
Berlin Stock Exchange is a huge two-storey floodlit
excavation, and 500 staff are busily moving into the
RAC headquarters in Bristol.

It is therefore very difficult to cast my mind back
to my student days in the early 1960s. I do remember
the cold beauty of Edinburgh seen from my battered
1933 open-top car passing through the formal
geometry of the New Town. I ground in low gear past
the Castle, shrouded in mist, to the fine red sandstone
Art School perched on the edge of the poorer district
of the Grass Market.

At Edinburgh there was still a strong tradition of
detailing in natural stone and wood and I received a
good grounding in full-size details. We stretched our
own paper, mixed our own ink, drew with ruling pens
and did our ink washes with camel hair brushes. We
studied the laws of sciagraphy and perspective carrying
out many working examples. I also attended lectures
at the University where we were given an excellent
grounding in history.

What was missing at Edinburgh, however, was the
conceptual challenge that I found at the Architectural
Association when I entered the third year in 1962.
That time was an 'anti-drawing' period, which was very
refreshing after Edinburgh where the cry of 'It's a nice
sheet, laddie' would greet a good drawing, irrespective
of its intellectual content. My tutors at the AA were, as

'Construction Esquisse'
drawn by Nick Grimshaw
at Edinburgh Art College
in 1960.

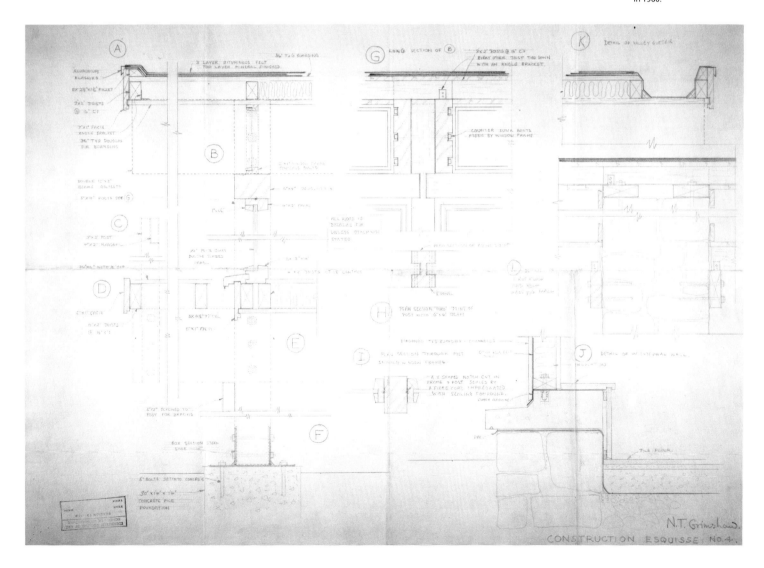

PLAN
A

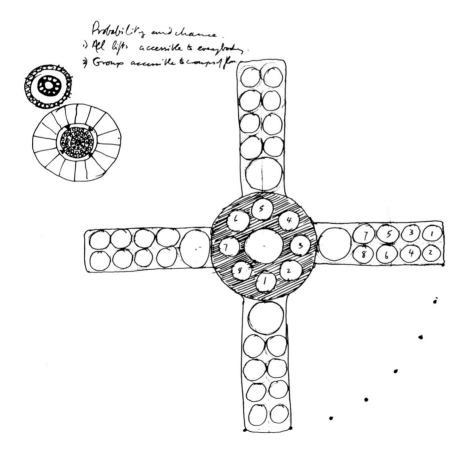

25 PERSONS PER 20'

SAY 1 LIFT PER 25 PEOPLE.
'PRACTICAL'
MAX. HEIGHT FOR PLAN A

IS 20 × 33 FT.
= 660 FT.
HOUSING 25 × 33 people

25
66
165
825 people.

This is allowing 200 □' p' person.

gives an approximate
height of 14 to 1 (660/60)

18

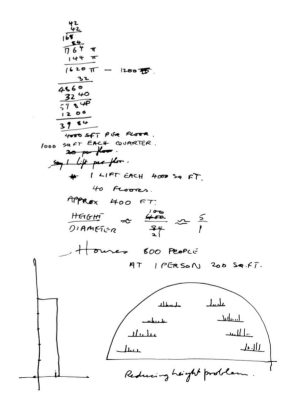

Probability and chance.
1) All lifts accessible to everybody.
2) Group accessible to groups of floors.

4000 SFT PER FLOOR.
1000 SQ FT EACH QUARTER.
20 per floor.
Say 1 lift per floor.
1 LIFT EACH 4000 SQ FT.
40 FLOORS.
APPROX 400 FT.

HEIGHT / DIAMETER ≈ 400 / 84/2 ≈ 5/1

Houses 800 PEOPLE
AT 1 PERSON 200 SQ.FT.

Reducing height problem.

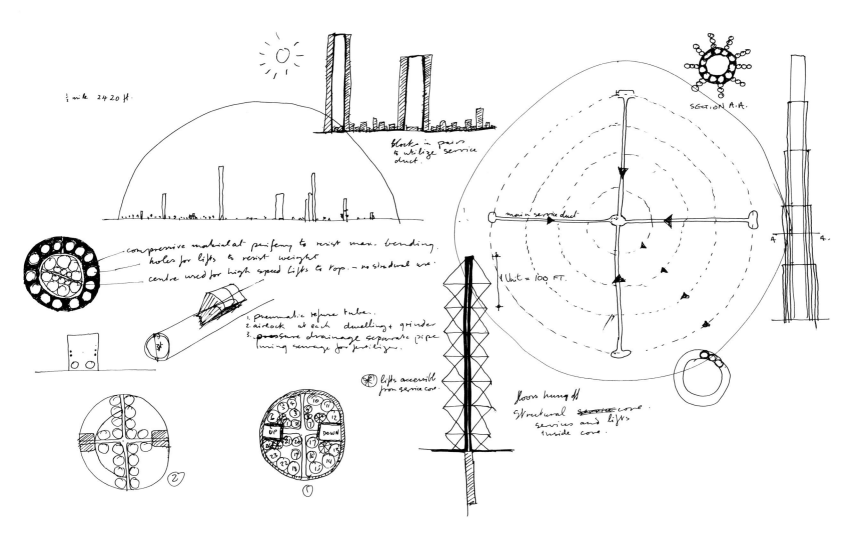

½ mile   2420 ft.

blocks in pairs
to utilize service
duct.

SECTION A·A.

compressive material at periery to resist max. bending.
holes for lifts to resist weight
centre used for high speed lifts to top. — no structural use.

main service duct

1 Unit = 100 FT.

1. pneumatic refuse tubes.
2. airlock at each dwelling + grinder
3. pressure drainage separate pipe
using sewage for fertilizer.

✳ lifts accessible
from service core.

floors hung off
structural service core.
services and lifts
inside core.

UP   DOWN

A.   A.

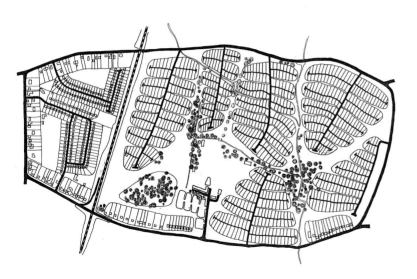

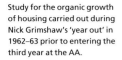

Study for the organic growth of housing carried out during Nick Grimshaw's 'year out' in 1962–63 prior to entering the third year at the AA.

I recollect, Anthony Wade, Alvin Boyarsky, John Winter, Roy Landau and Stamford Anderson. Archigram had a considerable influence then but was strongly attacked by many. Cedric Price was in his usual role, contributing a great deal but not really admitting to being a tutor. It was a lively and thought-provoking time.

The challenge in the field of ideas at the AA was more than substantial. It was a time when you could write your own programmes and in many ways direct your own studies. However, the inability to present your case and complete your project in time meant having 'Fail' written on your jury report. I believe that the conceptual toughness, which can be seen in many of the projects in this book, owes a lot to the dialogue I have always tried to instill in the Nicholas Grimshaw & Partners office, where ideas have to be defended in the same rigorous way as was the norm at the AA in the early 1960s.

I have seen several themes emerging from my time at the AA, and my work as a practising architect since 1965, which include: the relationship between living and working; geometrical order; the relationships between architecture, structure and services; a fundamental belief in people's right to manipulate their own surroundings; energy and world resources; and, finally, detail – the way things work and are put together.

Coming, as this book does, 30 years into my architectural career, I thought it might be worthwhile to elaborate on these themes, to trace some of my early sketches and drawings in relation to them, and to relate the themes to projects completed during this early period of 1967 to 1988, through my own work and that of the office.

I first raised the issue of the relationship between living and working and the quality of life in a project we were set at the AA in 1963, which was my first effort at designing an office building. The building was to occupy a site on Tottenham Court Road in London; it is quite interesting to look at the office building there today – which is now in a very bad state of repair – and reflect on the criticisms which many architects received at the time. In commenting on the standard type of office building that we were being asked to produce, I said:

This kind of office environment brings into question the whole problem of work/living relationships. Given modern communications, would not the vast majority of office work be (a) automated, or (b) of a more executive and creative level; if (b) pertains, then much higher environmental conditions would be required and some sort of integration between office and living on a 24-hour cycle is implied. In this case, why London? Surely there is room here for questioning the whole process of working in cities.

As students we returned to this theme again and again, particularly in our housing projects. This was the time of Jane Jacobs' *The Death and Life of Great American Cities* and a lot of debate took place about the merits of building housing schemes which were separate entities from the city and bore little relation to the traditionally accepted values of living and working in close proximity. Planners were busy classifying inner city industry as 'non-conforming' use and grants were given to businesses to move out to new towns and industrial estates. This seems ironic today when many London boroughs and major cities in England are desperately trying to create industry in their midst.

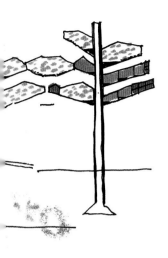

Studies showing 'organic
growth' carried out in
1964–65, as part of Nick
Grimshaw's thesis for an
'Urban University' during his
final year at the AA.

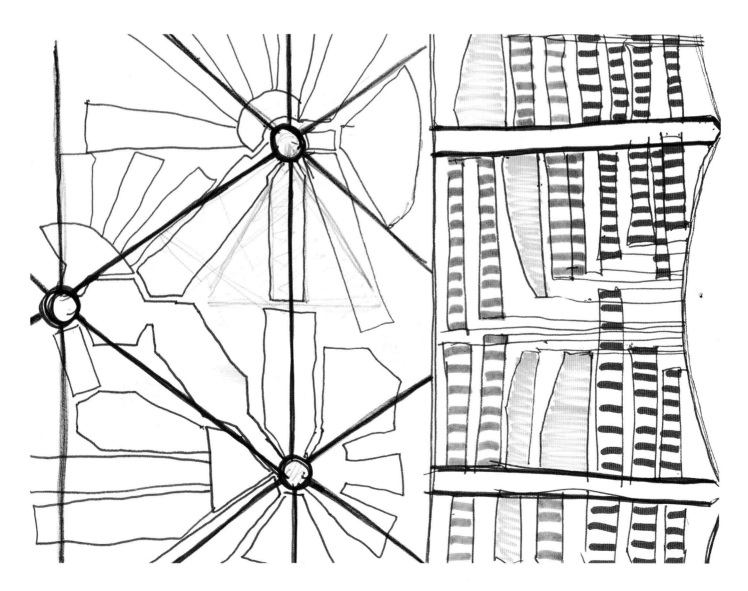

Autobiographical note

Studies carried out during
Nick Grimshaw's thesis year at
the AA in 1964–65. Here
he was working on combining
an efficient 60° movement
grid with an orthogonal
building grid for his 'Urban
University' project.

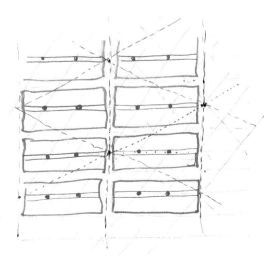

When the practice came to work on schemes for industrial parks at Aztec West and Gillingham, we tried hard to suggest ways in which housing and residential areas could be integrated with industry, but without great success. In an article in the *RIBA Journal* of October 1980, I used Charles Eames' house in Pacific Palisades as an example of an open-framed structure which could be occupied for either industrial or residential use. I pointed out the enormous savings that could be made, particularly in energy, but also in social cost in trying to integrate the two activities. I put forward a prototype framework building of 10,000m² which showed a complete mix of industry, residential, leisure, education and all other aspects of everyday living happening under one roof. I later developed this idea that in creating a relationship between living and working, we would be paying greater attention to the quality of life in general. In his book, *A Pattern Language,* Christopher Alexander expounds on this subject:

If you spend eight hours of your day at work and eight hours at home, there is no reason why your work place should be any less of a community than your home … Anyone who uses the phrase 'where do you live' in its everyday sense accepts as his own the widespread cultural awareness of the fact that no one really lives at his place of work – there is no song or music there, no love, no food – that he is not alive while working, not living, only toiling away and being dead. As soon as we understand this situation it leads at once to outrage. Why should we accept a world in which eight hours of the day are 'dead'? Why should we not create a world in which our work is as much part of life, as much alive as anything we do at home with our family and with our friends?

It seems to me that very little progress has been made on this issue of bringing living and working closer together, although in inner cities in London and elsewhere there seems to be a much greater interest in living in the centre and bringing industry back to the city. Traditionally industries occurred throughout London under railway arches and in mews in residential areas and these are now being encouraged again. The drift of people away from the office and towards the home has been much slower than we all anticipated in the 1960s. However, high office rents and the savage cut backs due to the recession of the last five years have caused many firms to experiment with the idea of people working from home. Computers can be linked to a head office by modem, and fax machines are becoming common in many households. Pioneer courses have been set up in De Montfort University at Milton Keynes, for example, where all the students are supplied with computers with direct links from their homes to the university.

The second theme I want to turn to is the question of geometrical order. At the time of leaving the AA, my thesis centred around the whole question of grids and the relationships between them. In particular I spent many hours working on the relationship between a movement grid, which was at 60°, and the development of 'spaces', which I felt had to be on a 90° grid – there seemed to be no logic in designing buildings with 60° corners. One or two buildings were designed on that basis at the time – Reading Town Hall, I believe, was one

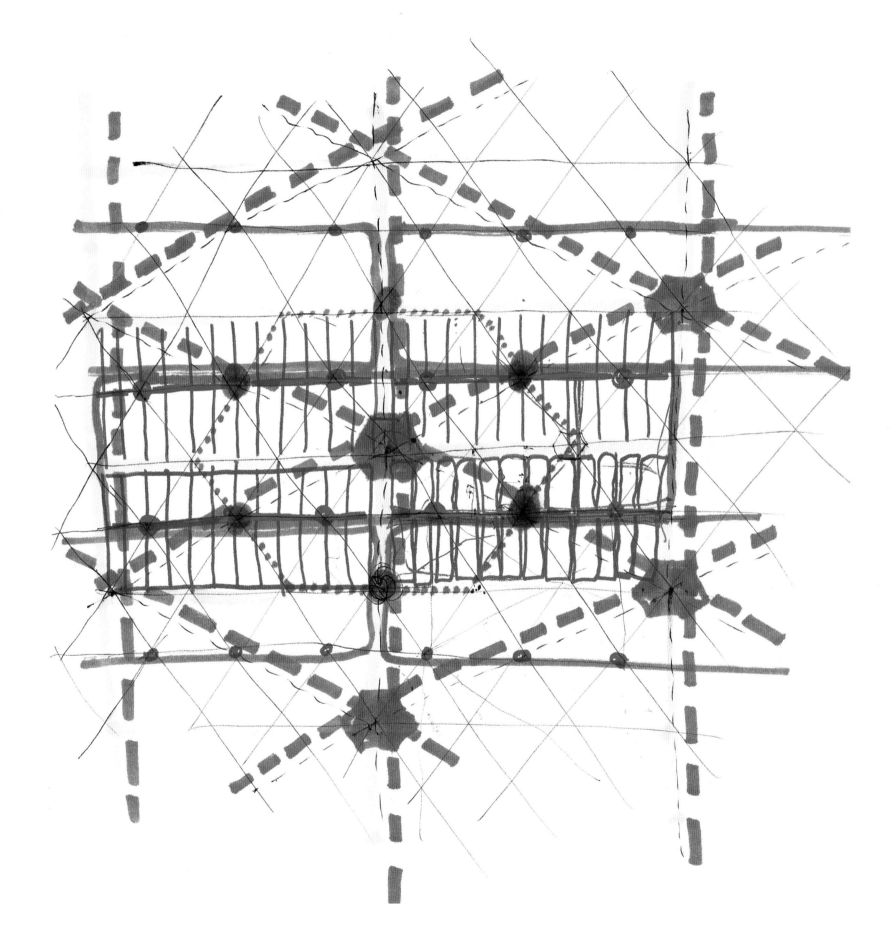

A cardboard model made for Nick Grimshaw's thesis illustrating how the system for an urban university could be constructed from a limited range of components. This overall view (left) and the detail and plan view (opposite page) show the influence of Jean Prouvé's thinking on Grimshaw's designs.

and Berlin (Tegel) Airport another. The movement grid acted as a linking network across the whole Covent Garden area – which was at that time assumed to be a major redevelopment area with most of the buildings being demolished. The 'Urban University', which was the subject of my thesis, occupied a 120-acre site on a 90° grid linked with the 60° grid through nodal points for movement. These movement towers also had complementary service towers, so the whole vast system was set up on the basis of structural towers on a 60° grid which in turn supported flexible development above.

At the same time as working on this highly theoretical concept of movement and structure, I was writing a history thesis on Hippodamus of Miletus who was sometimes referred to as 'the father of the grid'. The idea was that a theoretical grid thrown over a landscape, which itself was not necessarily level, could act as a marvellous ordering discipline for development to take place. I followed this idea through many examples and, in particular, at Priene and Olynthus where I was able to trace the order right through to the rooms in an individual house. This concept of an overall order which could be manipulated is a theme which has stayed with me. The subtlety in development of this idea is that even though the organizational concept may be fairly strong, it is only an abstract or geometrical idea and there is a great freedom for the individual to express himself. This is in complete contrast to current ideas of so-called 'urban planning', where attempts are made to match buildings stylistically or contextually with no real interest being shown in the overall order of things.

The third theme, one which relates to my own work over the years as well as the current work of the practice, follows directly on from the idea of geometrical order. It is to do with the structure of buildings and the way they are serviced. I mentioned above the service towers which played such an important role in my thesis for the university at Covent Garden. I was lucky enough to receive a commission immediately after leaving the AA which consisted of the conversion into a hostel of six Victorian houses, which at the time were completely unserviced and in a very bad state of repair. It was an opportunity to put theory into practice; and the idea, which can be seen in my original thumbnail sketch, was to stand a service tower behind the buildings and thus provide all the bathroom and sanitary accommodation needed for 200 students.

This tower bore out the concept that servicing should always be ancillary to buildings. The buildings have now changed in use and the tower, which was no longer needed, has been dismantled. However, the idea of having a structure with independent servicing is something that can be found as a theme through many of the practice's early projects. Service towers can be seen at the industrial scheme at Nottingham in the form of sleek green fibreglass tubes, and in the factory for Vitra where they carried all the staircases, bathroom accommodation and the servicing elements which were ancillary to the main production space.

The expression of structure became an increasingly important part of our work during the period up to 1988. In the early industrial work, the structures were relatively simple column and beam arrangements, albeit

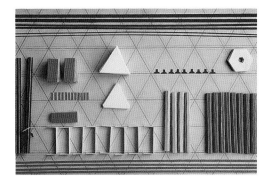

with the stresses, detailing and speed of erection being thought out in great detail. Later on, where wider spans were required, such as for Oxford Ice Rink or the superstore for Sainsbury's in Camden Town, the structure almost became the building. The two great masts suspending the roof and creating a completely clear space for the ice rink gave the whole scheme a dramatic image and, in a sense, created the architecture. With Sainsbury's, where we were seeking to return to the 'market hall' concept, we felt it essential that the way the structure worked should be appreciated from the outside of the building; this can be seen in the ends of the cantilevered beams which support the main arches in a constant rhythm along the principal elevation, and the tie downs which in turn support the other end of the cantilever clearly expressed along the street frontage. Intense thought and care went into the way this building fitted into the street scene, ensuring that the structural rhythm and scale complemented the Georgian houses on the opposite side of the street.

I believe that there are very few universally-admired buildings where the detailing is not superb; I think it would be possible to say the same thing about structure. It is hard to think of any good building where the structure is not at least understandable in terms of the architect's knowledge of the spanning capabilities of the materials available to him, and it is possible, of course, to find many instances of fine architecture which lean heavily on structure for their architectural expression.

The fourth theme which I want to follow is the principle that people should have the right to organize

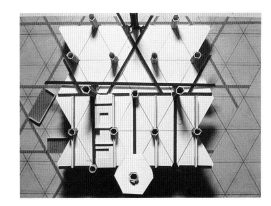

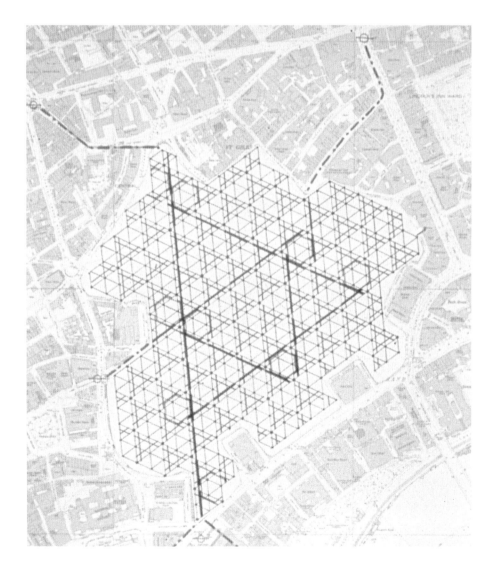

The final layout of Nick Grimshaw's thesis for an 'Urban University' set in the Covent Garden area of London. The heavy blue lines show travolator routes through the network.

and control their own surroundings. This was a fundamental consideration for me when doing my thesis project for the Covent Garden university. The ability to manipulate and change the surroundings was such a strong issue that I felt the only way to express it was to put it on film. I made an animated film by setting a 16mm camera vertically above a plan view of the project. I shot a few frames, moved all the elements fractionally, and then shot a few more frames – carrying on all through one day and night, ending up with very sore knees. However, it did give a very good picture of how I saw the growth and change of the university taking place over the years. It was not change for the sake of change; rather, the human force behind the university and the changing nature of its activities would motivate the adaptations within the structure and servicing of the building. What I wrote then was fairly extreme and I feel perhaps my views have since become a little more defined. Nevertheless, I quote the paragraph which described the essence of the scheme:

To accept the status quo of monolithic brick and concrete, of immovable, inflexible extensions of the earth's crust, of little higher environmental standard than caves and then to continually try to torture them to today's needs, is to continuously slide away from the problem. It is my hope that it is not buildings we will be designing in the future, it is organisms capable of variation and adaptation with as large a range as the technology of the minute permits. We will be dealing with all the sensory effects our minds can encompass – heat, light, sound, texture, muscle sense, etc. We will be designing the instruments and writing the score for perhaps only one performance. Perhaps a script for a day, a month, a year and all the time we must be prepared to scrap, to adapt, to add to our environment with all the means at our disposal.

This university project is a tentative step towards providing a new kind of environment which throws heavy responsibility on the user. I do not accept the view that society will seek greater and greater sublimation of its senses when released from mechanical and repetitive tasks. It is my firm belief that the individual will begin to realize his own potential and develop it. Once this is achieved society will be making far greater demands on its sensory and psychological environment, demands which are not even acknowledged by the majority of designers.

I was greatly encouraged in this project by my tutors Cedric Price and Peter Cook, and also by Gordon Pask who was involved in the new science of cybernetics. He saw parallels between the way in which the university changed and the way natural organisms adapted themselves to their surroundings.

There is certainly a campaigning element about these words, but it is perhaps worth noting that the aim was 'to give power to the people'. I was against monumentality and the idea of forcing buildings on people who had no say in their design. This was perhaps a reaction against the 'concrete jungles' being created in the 1960s – the rather poorly constructed office blocks and housing schemes which we have seen coming down in the 1980s.

I first had the opportunity to demonstrate some ideas on flexibility with the block of flats at Park Road where

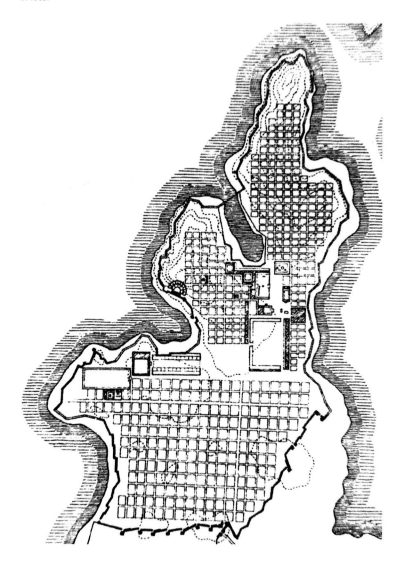

Plan of Miletus which formed
the cover of Nick Grimshaw's
history thesis at the AA
in 1965.

alternative flat plans were discussed with the owners of
the co-operative and agreement reached on those
preferred. The building was nevertheless conceptually
very clear, in that the flats could be changed or
reorganized in very many different forms over the life of
the building.

The possibility of a workforce in a factory building
being able to affect their surroundings first manifested
itself in the design of the building for Herman Miller
at Bath. Herman Miller's philosophy was, of course,
already firmly rooted in the idea of flexibility. They were
the first producers of open plan furniture systems and
made great play of the idea that users of a building
could change their environment by moving around
screens, furniture and all the basic elements of their
internal environment. The proposal I put to them was
that the building should continue this idea; it should be
able to reflect the activities going on inside it and
accommodate a wide degree of variation. They liked this
idea and the fact that the building was conceived as
being fundamentally non-monumental. In fact, the
building has been altered quite considerably over the
years and the exterior has certainly reflected the
changes that have gone on within it. It has also always
been a popular building with the workforce. I feel this
supports my philosophy that a building has presence
and lasting quality not because of what it is, but
because of what it does. If it serves its purpose well and
is liked by the occupants and those who pass by, then it
will always have a life of its own.

The practice pursued this idea of flexibility with
industrial buildings at Winwick Quay where a number of
small industries were to be grouped together under one

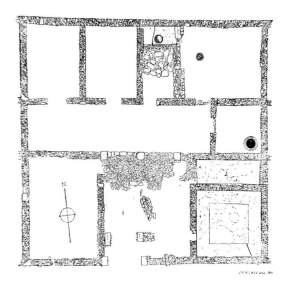

umbrella roof. Here the cladding itself was flexible and could accommodate entrance doors, loading doors and glazing anywhere within its grid. The main services were located in a ring around the building so that secondary connections could enter from the outside through hoods at any point on the perimeter.
As a direct result of this flexible servicing concept, we developed a specially-designed stainless steel bathroom module that could be moved by a forklift truck to any position within the building, depending on the user's requirements.

The fifth theme I want to give some attention to is the question of world resources. In 1965, we were all very influenced and moved to hear Buckminster Fuller speak in London to launch his ideas for a world design science decade. His message was inspiring, revolving not in simplistic terms around peace or war, but in scientific terms around the idea of the distribution of resources. He referred to 'the haves and the have-nots' at a time before the concept of 'third world' was being talked about. His idea was that most conflicts in the past had been caused by the desire for resources and that their more equal distribution would make for a much more peaceful world. He felt that those of us who had design skills should use them to try to produce enclosures and facilities and servicing mechanisms that could be used by the millions of 'have-nots'. He linked this with the idea of mass production, and thus led us on to concepts of engineering, the way cars were produced, and how people could put their own environments together with a 'kit of parts'. He was also concerned about the amount of energy used to produce materials and, more especially, about the concept of waste.

Extract from the plan of Olynthus also showing an enlargement of an individual house.

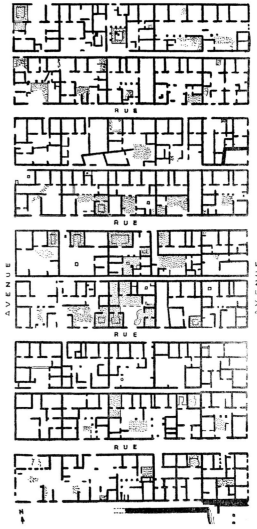

Autobiographical note

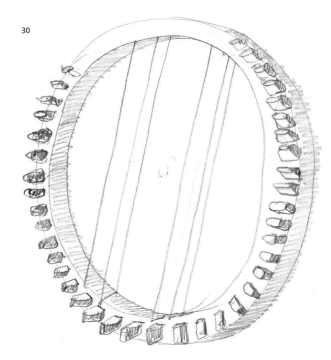

For his 'Measured Drawing' requirement at the AA in 1963, Nick Grimshaw carried out studies of a windmill in Greece. This sketch shows the main vertical drive wheel with wooden teeth engaging on the smaller horizontal cog which in turn rotated the mill stone.

Overall sketch of the vertical drive wheel of the windmill in Greece.

When Bucky returned to London in 1967, he visited the recently completed service tower and I was fascinated by the way in which he could range from the most minute engineering details to the whole concept of linking new mechanisms to old structures.

Other great influences at that time were innovators such as Jean Prouvé who devoted his life to the idea of producing components in an elegant way to be used on many buildings, not simply one-off elements for use on a particular project. This concept was also followed through by Charles Eames. In his furniture designs, a kind of democracy reigned in that, with a mass-produced item, anyone who could afford it could have it.

Since these early influences in the 1960s, we have of course been affected by the energy crisis, and this struck a chord in me from the point of view of the wastefulness of travel. In this connection I was able to raise, once again, the notion of living and working closely together. When I spoke at the RIBA Energy Conference in 1979, I calculated that the fuel used by the workforce of a typical 8,000m² building travelling two miles to work would be enough to heat the building for a year; and if they lived ten miles away, heat the building for five years.

World resources are still a fundamental issue today, and the question of industrialized nations helping underdeveloped countries is a real issue, both in political and financial terms. It is not generally thought that designers can help in this dialogue but I think they can make a fundamental contribution, as much by designing objects as by providing know-how. It may well be that one of the major exports from industrialized countries over the coming years will not be artefacts but skills.

The sixth theme I want to examine is the question of detail. I think I can say that I have always been interested in the way things work, but it was not until I went to architecture school that I began to take an interest in the way buildings were put together. I mentioned earlier how building construction was taught at Edinburgh; later, at the AA, one of the requirements as part of the overall course was to produce a measured drawing. I was opposed to the idea of measuring the facade of a building and reproducing it as a flat elevation, and I was determined to try to use this project as a way of understanding how something worked. I left the issue unresolved but, on holiday in Greece in 1962, I came across the most marvellous working windmill. I measured it and studied its machinery in the greatest detail. One of the things that intrigued me most was the fact that the building was 200 years old and yet all the working parts had been designed to allow their replacement without dismantling the windmill as a whole. This made a deep impression on me. I realized that this building had probably had every moving part in it replaced several times during its lifetime, and that these would probably be replaced many times again in the future.

Detail, I suppose, has been the essence of my work since leaving the AA. I have already touched on the service tower which was my first job. I designed every detail and did the drawings myself, as well as visiting all the subcontracting firms. I developed an understanding of the importance of the process by which things were made and the pointlessness of doing drawings or specifications for products which could not be produced. This interest in detail has continued through

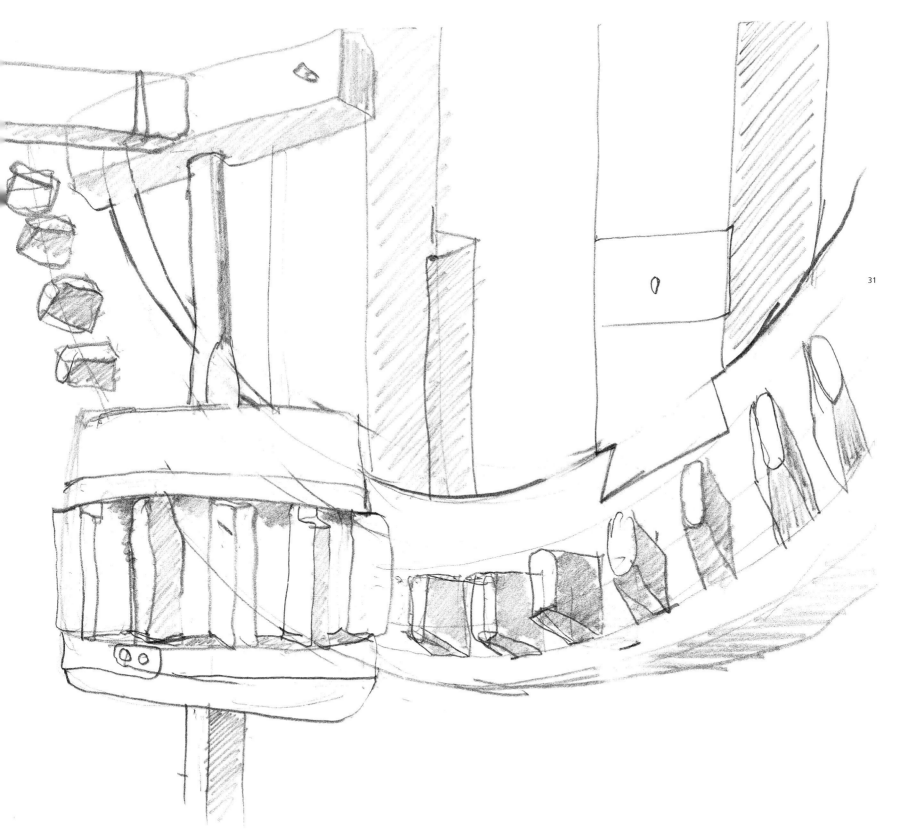

Autobiographical note

32 Drive shaft of the windmill in Greece. Small pieces of hardwood were strapped around the shaft to reduce wear.

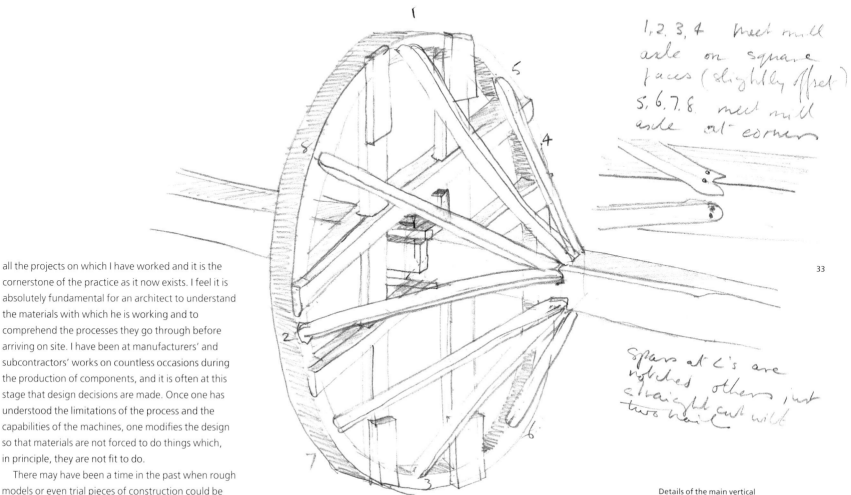

all the projects on which I have worked and it is the cornerstone of the practice as it now exists. I feel it is absolutely fundamental for an architect to understand the materials with which he is working and to comprehend the processes they go through before arriving on site. I have been at manufacturers' and subcontractors' works on countless occasions during the production of components, and it is often at this stage that design decisions are made. Once one has understood the limitations of the process and the capabilities of the machines, one modifies the design so that materials are not forced to do things which, in principle, they are not fit to do.

There may have been a time in the past when rough models or even trial pieces of construction could be done and craftsmen could be relied upon to interpret them to produce a good quality of building. However that time has passed. If we are to see fine architecture around us, an understanding of detail and the production of good drawings is paramount.

I think it was this passionate desire to convince people of the importance of detail that first brought the practice to the idea of having an exhibition. Models and prototypes were assembled from all over the country, sketch details were unearthed and, in January 1988, the practice held a major exhibition in the Florence Hall of the RIBA, showing most of the projects featured in this volume.

The Product and Process Exhibition welcomed tens of thousands of visitors in spite of its short duration; there were visitors from 17 countries – everyone from parties of schoolchildren to delegations from British industry. The intention was to tell the story of how the

Details of the main vertical drive wheel.

Above left to right: houses built into cliffs at Vouvray, France; Loire Château garden, France; mud-brick house, Morocco, applying clay to the walls.

buildings were created – from the initial concept sketches to the care and attention involved in creating the details. The practice's collaboration with engineers like Ove Arup and Anthony Hunt had shown our ability to work at a large scale on buildings such as Homebase and Oxford Ice Rink covering up to 5,000m² of column-free space. I think it was this ability to understand and appreciate structural design, and the careful attention to detail, that subsequently drew Jane Priestman (then head of design at British Rail) to commission our team to design the new International Terminal at Waterloo.

This was also the time that the scaffolding was just being removed from the Financial Times Printing Works revealing what many saw as a heroic facade some 140m long and 16m high – itself perhaps evocative of some of the great railway architecture of the 19th century.

Because of the commission for Waterloo, the practice's workload increased rapidly both in scale and intensity – at one point employing 92 people. During this period of growth from 1988 to 1994, I travelled widely lecturing and visiting the work of other architects. I felt this allowed me to greatly broaden my horizons and, consequently, a further four themes became apparent in the work of the practice: a sense of landscape and context; a feeling for the quality and meaning of materials; a sense of space and the feeling of movement through it; and a sense of history.

I should like to try to develop these themes in the light of my travels and also to discuss how my interests in other cultural areas have affected me and the work of the office over the last few years.

Travel has undoubtedly heightened my awareness of the sense of landscape and context – what Giancarlo di Carlo calls the 'spirit of the place'. Since the early 1970s, I have regularly visited Francis Van de Velde who lives in a modest manor house in Tours, surrounded by barns built in the beautiful local limestone. This is certainly a region where natural landscape and geometry somehow work in complete harmony. At Chambourcy in the summer, the strictly-ordered parterre gardens, with vegetables planted in immaculate patterns, make a marvellous contrast with the undulating pathways. In winter, one can see the natural spectacle of the Loire in full flood packed with ice and with snow on its banks.

The other reason for returning to Tours year after year was the Fête de la Musique at the Grange de Meslay. This was run by the Van de Velde family and enabled me to meet musicians such as Sviatoslav Richter, Radu Lapu, Daniel Barenboim, Pierre Boulez and many others. The festival took place in a 13th century barn, the construction of which would be an inspiration to any architect, let alone one whose roots are deeply influenced by structure.

On many occasions I visited a wine grower in Vouvray who lived with his ancient mother in a house constructed in the hollowed out limestone cliffs which left a very strong impression. It was perhaps this almost total integration of landscape and building that inspired the design of the building for Editions Van de Velde, which evolved as a low construction in glass and green fibreglass to harmonize with the naturally very bright greens seen throughout the region.

It was soon after the exhibition in 1988 that I bought our ruined barn on the edge of the salt-marshes

and sand dunes in Norfolk. I am sure that the soft wind-blown forms of the dunes, and the succession of immensely long horizontal sand banks separated by slivers of sea, had a great influence on me. It was as though nature was introducing me to the curve. The way the Western Morning News building hugs the contours of its hillside, for example, and indeed the organic form of Waterloo, have echoes of the natural curves found in the countryside and on the sea shore. The great fascination for me, though, was to be able to transpose these curves into geometry.

The instinctive mathematics of boat building also became a fascination in Norfolk. I formed a great respect for a young boat builder in Wells which resulted in the total restoration of Norfolk Sharpie No 57. The three-dimensional curves which are commonplace in boat building can now be seen, largely due to the practice's computer capability, to be emerging in many of our projects.

It was during the 1980s that I first started skiing. I never achieved any kind of mastery of the slopes but the snowy landscape, and particularly the very subtle curves seen in the morning light and as the sun was setting, seemed to introduce to me a new vocabulary to be overlaid on conventional orthogonal geometry. My first visit to Finland was also made at this time and I became aware of the extremely subtle way in which landscape seemed to be built into the consciousness of the Finns. Aalto's sanatorium at Paimio, for example, demonstrated a marvellous integration with the pine forests surrounding it.

I cannot leave the subject of landscape without discussing my time in Spain. In 1989, the practice won the competition to design the British Pavilion for Expo 92 in Seville. As well as exploring the small and magical Seville courtyards, which are like little oases of greenery, we visited what is perhaps the greatest piece of formal landscape in Europe – the Generalife gardens in Granada. Here one can experience not only the most marvellous use of water, but also a complex relationship between formal geometry on plan integrated with the contours of a steeply sloping hillside. The planting was wonderful; the ancient hedges genuinely formed outdoor rooms which, in the climate of Spain, seemed totally appropriate.

No building can be designed without some acknowledgement of its place, and alongside this greater understanding of landscape which I hope now runs through my office is, I believe, a greater appreciation of the significance of urban context. The development of a whole block in Camden for Sainsbury's was the practice's first really urban scheme and we tried hard to respond to the scale and rhythm, the light and shade, of the surrounding buildings. Again, travel and lecturing has honed these reflexes. The grain and scale of the alleyways and buildings in Seville, of grand open spaces like St Mark's Square in Venice, or an appreciation of the true urbanity of Lisbon, have all had their effect, as has the wonderful organic unity of Prague, unscathed by the ravages of war.

My understanding of the quality and meaning of materials has grown during my travels of the last few years and this experience, together with that of reconstructing the barn in Norfolk, has helped me to enlarge and enrich the palette of materials generally used by the office.

Above left to right: Eames House by Charles and Ray Eames, Pacific Palisades, California, 1949; Johnson Wax Administration Center by Frank Lloyd Wright, Racine, Wisconsin, 1936; Norfolk Sharpie No 57.

Above left to right: fountain at Villa Lante, Rome; paving in Seville; Park Güell, Barcelona.

My trip to Finland allowed me to see Aalto's famous House of Culture at first hand. Its curving brick wall needs to be seen by all who believe that brick is a formal orthogonal material. There is a richness in that building which goes far beyond the simple materials of its construction. As well as many of Aalto's buildings, I also visited Eliel Saarinen's country house, to which he and his compatriots retreated having won seven competitions in a row. Here timber and stone were used in a timeless way with round wooden columns and massive stone retaining walls.

When visiting Japan in 1993, I was enthralled by the use of timber. Again a whole new vocabulary was there to be absorbed, but it would take a number of visits and many sketches and photographs before even scratching the surface. The thing that most struck me was the homogeneous nature of many of the buildings, particularly at Kyoto. Not only were all the major structural elements in timber, often massive baulks of pine, but the fine detail was also carved in the same material. The joints were fascinating, not least because they could all be undone to allow new timbers to be introduced replacing those that had rotted in Japan's wet and humid climate.

One factor which links my interest in landscape and context with the quality of materials is that of 'ground space'. The ground floors of palazzi in Florence and Venice, or the Piccolomini Library of the cathedral in Siena, for example, literally spill out onto the streets and form marvellously textured areas of paving, often using different marbles and stone slabs. It may be the fear of frost damage that restrains the architects of Northern Europe, but cobbles and York stone

seem to be almost the limit of the palette here.

Turning to the subject of a sense of space and movement through spaces, there is nothing in my view to compare with arriving in Venice by boat and travelling along the canals at dusk. If this is done off season so that some mist is in the air, and if one's journey starts with the lagoon then moves onto the Grand Canal, then more minor canals, then the smallest waterways just giving separation between the buildings, the spatial and indeed the emotional and inspirational experience is complete.

It wasn't until the canalside houses in Camden that the practice had a complete fit-out to do, designing all the interiors. Until that time, most of our projects had been large-volume spaces with few subdivisions – although this doesn't mean that space, proportion, rhythm and structural order were not carefully considered; for example, the Oxford Ice rink viewing galleries allow a great appreciation of the space. The view from the high level entrance, having travelled up the gentle ramps outside, has been described as spatially spectacular. At the Camden Superstore, where for the first time a Sainsbury's supermarket had a curved ceiling, establishing a strong spatial identity in a project for such a tough and commercial client was considered to be quite an achievement.

In contrast, the small scale of the canalside houses raised new considerations and caused us to reflect on how few really modern houses have been built in London or indeed in England since the war. The critic Martin Pawley applauded the 'ruthless modernism applied to the first truly high-tech houses to be built in London for years'; and went on to say that these houses

Above left to right:
Volkswagen factory;
19th century submarine;
Boeing 747.

'may represent the beginning of a watershed in English domestic architecture … these are the houses of the New Age. They are buildings with a job to do and they look like it'.

Certainly we tried to create a feeling of connection with the outside, with teak balconies opening off the studio living rooms and huge electrically-operated vertical sliding doors. We also tried to introduce the warmth of natural materials which were illuminated by catching a little of the southern sun through carefully profiled rooflights.

It was around this time that I visited Aalto's own studio/house in Helsinki and I was able to talk with his wife, who was still referred to when changes or repairs were proposed for any of his buildings. What I particularly remember about Aalto's studio was that it was a peculiarly narrow space but beautifully lit partly by a small skylight in a sculptured opening. The main glazing opened onto a beautifully detailed, steeply-terraced courtyard, meticulously laid out with ferns and mosses. There was mastery here of inside/outside space. Certainly this consciousness of Aalto's work started to influence my thinking and that of the office – particularly when we were designing the Western Morning News building at Plymouth.

Following the Camden houses, this was the first building of any size where we had to design the complete interior. A grand atrium was conceived with many galleries opening from it, creating the hub of the building; small spaces, representing individual offices, were grouped around it. The open-plan spaces for the editorial staff were located directly behind the building's curved glazing thus overturning the normal spatial concept of placing individual offices on the perimeter.

Where larger volumes of space were concerned I well remember a visit to Norwich Cathedral with Max de Pree, the chairman of Herman Miller. He saw close analogies between the grand spaces created by the simple, repetitive, structural logic of English cathedrals and the kind of industrial structures he wanted to achieve.

The British Pavilion at Seville was conceived as a cathedral-like space, 25m from basement to roof and 70m by 37.5m on plan. Within this space a grand concourse floated; above it were the carefully positioned exhibition 'pods'. We conceived the idea of people *flowing* through the space, rather like a river, experiencing changing views through the great glass water-wall and from the various decks and exhibition levels, echoing the fabulous views over Seville from each turn of the cathedral tower.

There were many buildings at the Seville Expo which offered memorable spatial experiences, one of which, the Finnish pavilion, was a simple construction named after 'the devil's gorge' – where one passed between two structures, one a beautifully shaped boat-like piece representing Finnish crafts and the other a rectilinear steel pavilion representing Finnish high-tech industry. The resulting converging space was a brilliant creative achievement designed astonishingly by a group of third year architecture students. Another was the French pavilion where an artificial sky was created which seemed to be supported by the slenderest of columns. Under this was a glass floor which formed the roof of a grand three-dimensional

Above left to right:
Brighton railway station;
Paddington railway station,
London; Milan railway
station.

cinematic experience. It was possible to pass through this 3D effect by taking a travolator which dipped down from the deck level and up the other side. This pavilion, I believe, might be the forerunner of all kinds of future visual/spatial architectural experiences.

Currently two major projects are occupying the practice. Both of them are total pieces of architecture in that they are highly contextual and involve the design of the complete building down to its last detail. Both also have spatial qualities not hitherto seen in our work.

Firstly, the Waterloo International Terminal. Here the roof, now familiar to most Londoners, represents only 10% of the building in cost terms and maybe 15% in terms of space. The spaces below for arrivals and departures are known only to travellers. They are an exploration of the flow of people against the need for quiet resting places. Function is set against the perception of quality that will encourage people to accept the revolutionary concept of travelling to Europe by train. There are many precedents for these 'under spaces': Scharoun's Concert Hall for the Berlin Philharmonic, the Royal Festival Hall by Sir Leslie Martin et al and Aalto's House of Culture in Helsinki. None of these deal with the flow of people that we have had to envisage, but all – whether by lighting, sculptured shaping or simply the idea that no space is 'thrown away' – have influenced the way we have designed the spaces at Waterloo.

The Berlin Stock Exchange will be another milestone in the office's development. The building is an organic shape reaching deep into the site in order to maintain a

low profile on the Berlin skyline. However, the creation of a public concourse with views through all the spaces of the building does, I believe, break new ground in the spatial approach to public buildings.

At the time the practice was commissioned for Waterloo we were inevitably thrown into some kind of historical continuum. I was naturally aware of the marvellous inheritance of the great railway stations of the 19th century in this country – Paddington, Bristol, York, Brighton and, of course, St Pancras, in many ways the greatest of them all. However, we also needed to get into perspective some of the very fine stations in Europe, such as Leipzig, Cologne and Milan. I was equally aware that we were not just involved in an exciting new project with a fast-track programme, but that whatever we did would inevitably be European and part of its history. Our brief reinforced this – the building had to be designed to last for 125 years.

But what are the elements which make a building of lasting quality? Perhaps the only definition for this is that buildings will only survive if society feels they are relevant. I think it was Buckminster Fuller who said: 'A well-loved cardboard house will last for ever.' Most good architects design buildings which are relevant to their time and use the best materials available to them. They leave it to others to decide the fate of their buildings in the future and to look after their repair.

In my lectures, I sometimes show a slide of a mud-brick house with two people carefully renovating a wall by pressing handfuls of clay onto the surface. I also point out that the Roman pantiled roofs, so loved in the Mediterranean region and which so many people consider timeless, are under constant repair. The timber

rafters, the tiling fixings and the tiles themselves are replaced in an unconscious time-cycle which no-one has yet defined. This again recalls my study of the Greek windmill.

So far as Waterloo is concerned, the life-span of all the components has been assessed and they should be replaced or repaired before they fail – this is the case with Boeing 747s, for example, and should be the same for buildings. Glass can easily be replaced, by simply cutting out the silicon joints; neoprene gaskets can be removed and reinstated without dismantling the structure; and paint finishes – although of the highest durability available – can be renewed regularly. It does now appear that Waterloo International Terminal may be needed by society for many years to come; rail travel seems to have finally proved itself against the background of our congested roads and skies.

However, I believe that buildings, on the whole, are the servants of society. Some of the very best have been destroyed by man. Others, which perhaps have the ability to adapt and change, have lasted through many centuries.

In my own working life as an architect, I have seen my first building demolished. The service tower at Sussex Gardens was removed when the use of the buildings changed from a student hostel to a hotel with individual bathrooms for each room. Another has been moved – Ladkarn was dismantled and moved from the Docklands to Beckton Heights. Yet another, Herman Miller in Bath, has gone through radical changes. On the other hand, there have been attempts at a post-war listing for the block of flats at Park Road, which was designed as a minimum-cost building so that a group of young

professionals could have a roof over their heads. Indeed, the very flexible Herman Miller building is in danger of becoming some kind of monument to a new form of industrial democracy.

It is my belief and hope that buildings such as Oxford Ice Rink, Stockbridge Pool or the Sainsbury's Superstore, will always have a place in the society in which they find themselves. They may find other uses in the future but let us hope that the architecture will stand the test of time. Perhaps even the Financial Times Printing Works, which at the moment is so effectively performing its function, could eventually follow the example of Bankside Power Station, which is to be turned into a gallery of modern art, and be put to other cultural uses as the balance in society shifts from work to leisure.

Nicholas Grimshaw, London, November 1994

Above left to right: pantile roofs, Berne; street in Seville; Paimio Sanatorium by Alvar Aalto, Finland, 1929–33.

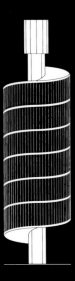

**Service Tower, Student Hostel,
London, 1967**

'This was my first project and it proved to be
as challenging as anything I have ever done.
The client, a charitable trust, had bought a row
of six 19th-century houses with the intention
of turning them into a hostel for 200 students.
The houses were grand in proportion but had
become totally derelict, they lacked even the
basic services. My idea was to build a "service
tower" to provide the bathrooms, showers
and wc's for all the students, accessible from
a continuous ramp, thus leaving the
maximum amount of space in the houses for
student rooms.

   'The steel-framed core of the tower went up
in three weeks. We then used it as a crane to
hoist in place all the bathrooms and sections
of helical ramp. By experimenting at the
steelwork factory, we found it was possible to
feed a strip of steel through rollers at an angle
and thus form a helix. This was geometry on
the shop floor – 20 years before we had CAD
in our office – and my first experience of
co-ordinating 35 specialist subcontractors
to produce a building quite innovatory for
its time.' **NG**

Previous page
Model showing the helical
ramp surrounding the
bathroom pods.

Top to bottom: the houses on
the corner of Sussex Gardens
and Westbourne Terrace
behind which the service
tower originally stood;
plan view of the houses
showing how all student
rooms had access to the
service tower; early sketch
model showing the service
tower in hexagonal form.

Opposite: Nick Grimshaw's
sketch of the service tower
drawn in 1965 soon after
leaving the AA.

42 Conversions can be challenging for architects as they
impose their own parameters that can often be
dictatorial. But out of the imposed difficulties can come
an inspired solution that may be seen in the future as a
paradigm worthy of imitation. To turn six 19th-century
terrace houses into a student hostel in the late 1960s
was no routine task. London houses of that date look
better from the street front than they do from behind.
There are always untidy rear accretions and additions by
succeeding generations in a variety of attempts at
modernization. Plumbing is usually the most noticeable
feature – a spaghetti of lead, copper and plastic
tenuously suspended from crumbling stock brick walls.

When Nicholas Grimshaw was commissioned with his
partner to convert these Paddington houses into
student accommodation for the Anglican International
Students Club, he proposed a radical solution to solve
the problem of supplying enough services – by
designing a tower of sanitation to be added to the back
of the houses. There were an average of four units on
each floor of the houses, a total of 35 altogether.
Enough bathrooms, lavatories and laundry rooms had to
be provided to serve all the rooms. These were
accommodated in the tower where they were linked by
a gently sloping helical ramp which allowed the user to
saunter up and down searching for an available facility.

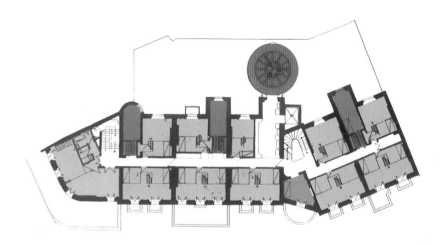

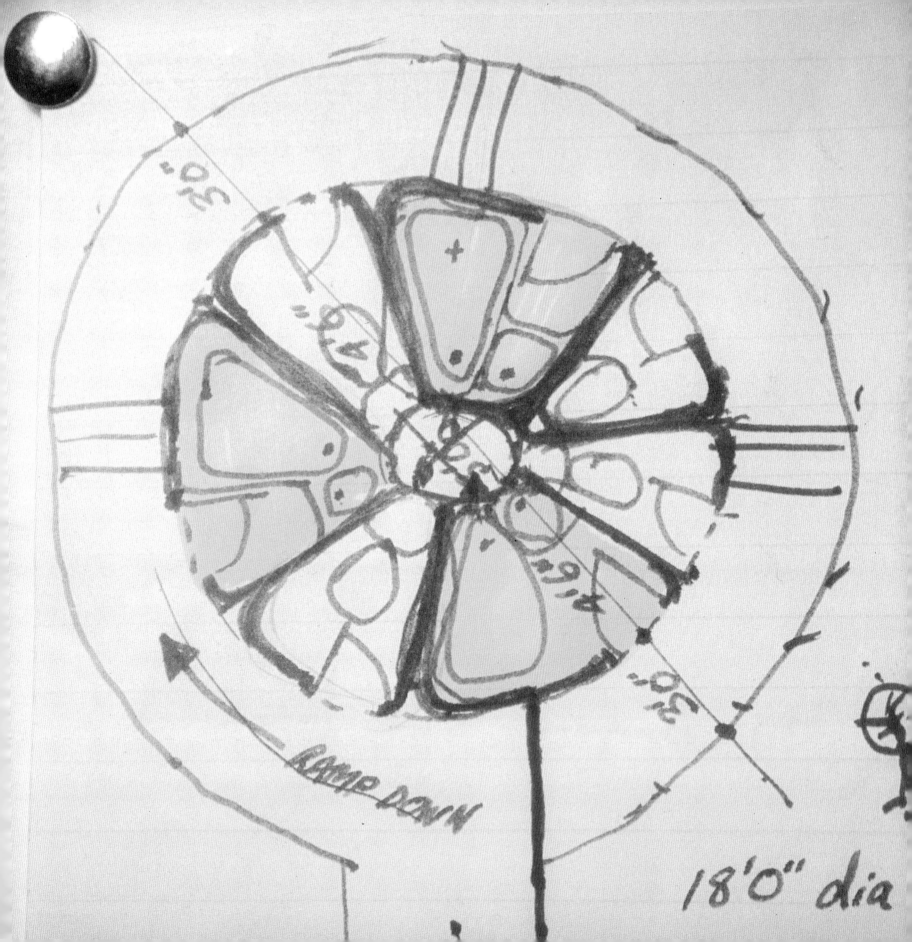

30'

6'0"

RAMP DOWN

30'

18'0" dia

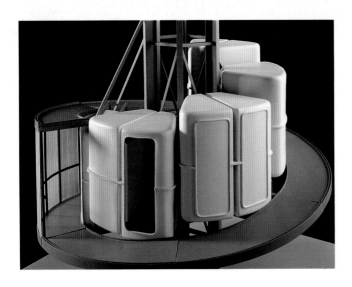

Sketch model of the service tower.

Construction of this service tower followed an original route by utilizing the central core of the tower as a crane. The bathroom 'pods' were made by a firm more used to making fibreglass dinghies. At the time of construction, the tower was described as a 'corn on the cob', because of its shape and the tightly packed nature of the capsules that appeared to grow from the steel stem. It was a seminal project of the late 1960s, and one that is today seen (despite its subsequent demolition) as an influential demonstration project from which many others have learned. It clearly had an impact, not just as an original idea and an inventive structure, but also as a pioneer example of the usefulness of the kit of parts idea. Kenzo Tange's Tokyo capsule hotel comes to mind, as does the more recent stair and lift towers at the Madrid Reina Sophia Museum.

View of the service tower under construction.

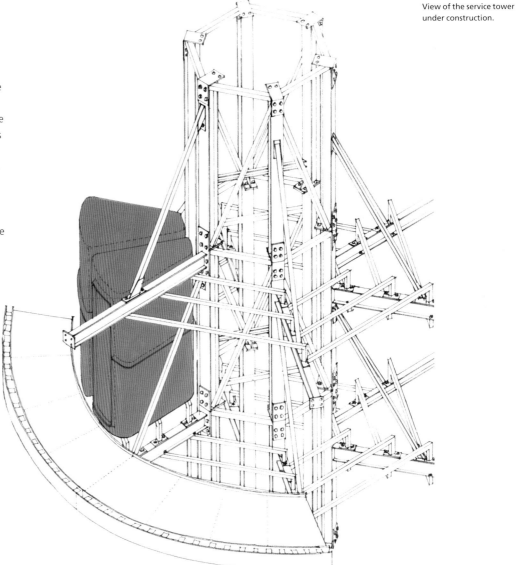

Structural sketch showing how the beams radiating at 60° from the central core were supported by diagonal hangars. The ramp units spanned between the ends of the radiating beams.

Architecture, Industry and Innovation

Top to bottom: bathroom pods being delivered to the site in Sussex Gardens; bathroom pods on the ground at basement level waiting to be hoisted into position; view looking upwards at the service tower during construction.

View of the steel structure of the service tower. This was erected in three weeks using the central core as a tower crane to put the rest of the structure in place.

There are many seeds of future designs to be seen in this project, and it is also revealing of the way that Grimshaw thought then and thinks today. As a student at the Architectural Association in the 1960s he inevitably came under the influence of the Archigram group, and in particular the teaching of Peter Cook. The idea of service towers linked to megastructures was very much a part of the thinking of the Archigram group. It was an idea that led to Richard Rogers' Lloyd's building in the City of London, and to the earlier Centre Georges Pompidou designed with Renzo Piano. Grimshaw shows in this early Paddington scheme that he absorbs and thinks about radical ideas and then, quietly and in his own way, makes innovation practical. He removed any trace of megalomania from the ideas of Archigram and humanized them.

This service tower was seen as very significant at the time and was published in *Architectural Design* in the very same issue as the pioneering History Faculty Library for the University of Cambridge by James Stirling. It almost acquired a temporary status not dissimilar to the Tatlin Tower – although Grimshaw's tower was literally rooted in function. All his early interest in technology is here, together with a belief in the practical application of prefabrication. It was an influential building and one glance at its simple and beautiful 'botanical' plan shows that it demonstrated an integrity in both form and functionality.

47

Service Tower, Student Hostel

Interior view of a bathroom pod.

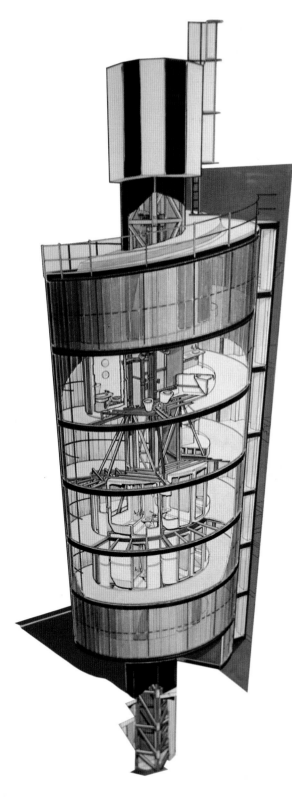

View of the service tower from the mews behind Sussex Gardens.

Cutaway perspective view of the service tower.

Light-hearted sketch by Grimshaw in 1965 envisaging a bathroom pod in full occupation.

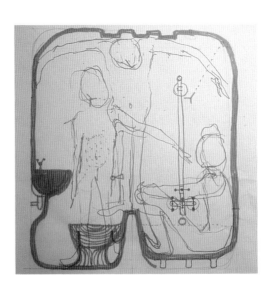

Architecture, Industry and Innovation

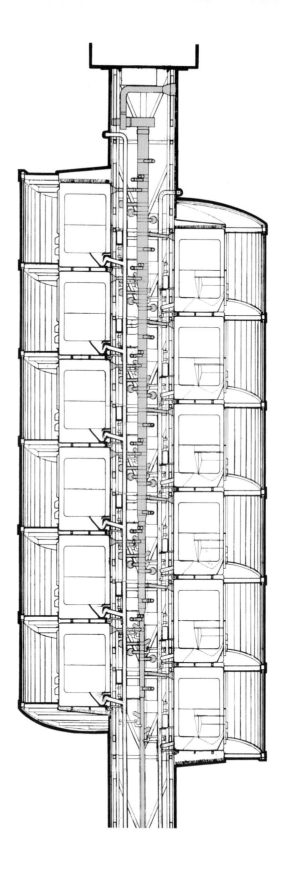

50 Section showing vertical
    waste stacks and main
    extractor ventilation duct.
    The duct increases in size
    towards the top of the tower
    terminating at a main fan unit
    with an extractor ventilation
    grille to the outside air.

0   2m

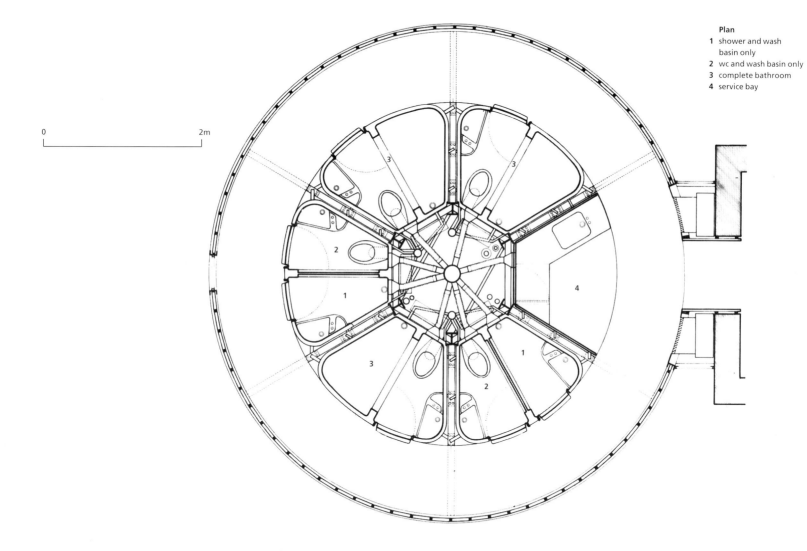

0   2m

Plan
1 shower and wash basin only
2 wc and wash basin only
3 complete bathroom
4 service bay

Service Tower, Student Hostel

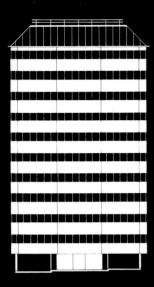

**Apartments, 125 Park Road,
London, 1968**

'We were a mixed group of professionals:
architects, surveyors, photographers, lawyers,
accountants and journalists. We were one of
the first groups of "co-owners" after the
Housing Corporation was formed. We wanted
to have a building which was cheap but gave
us the maximum amount of space and the best
possible views of Regent's Park. Industrial
buildings certainly looked better than the
pre-cast concrete housing schemes of the day
and I saw no reason why lightweight, long-
lasting materials could not be brought into
the residential field.

   'The idea that emerged was to have a
tower with a structural core of lift, stairs and
services and to make it possible to divide the
surrounding spaces in many different ways –
from 14 bed-sitting rooms to one massive flat
with two entrances. We lived in the building
for six years, enjoying the fantastic views over
the park. Changes in the layout are taking
place on a slower cycle than we thought, but
only recently two flats were combined to form
a magnificent L-shaped unit.' **NG**

Photomontage of the building, here seen from across the canal.

Nick Grimshaw's explanatory sketch of the cladding assembly.

54 **Previous page**
View looking up at the corner of the building.

Nick Grimshaw's explanatory sketch of the plan.

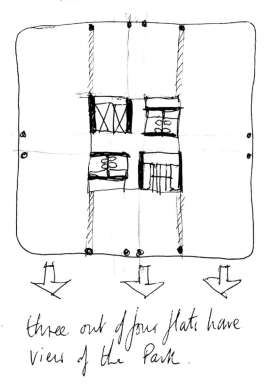

three out of four flats have views of the Park.

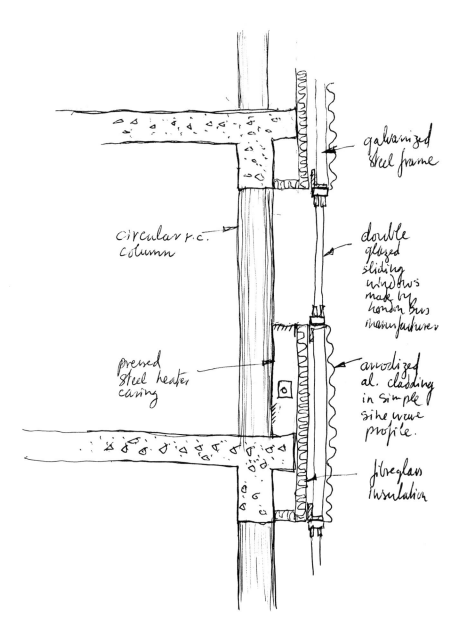

galvanized steel frame

circular r.c. column

double glazed sliding windows made by london bus manufacturer

pressed steel heater casing

anodized al. cladding in simple sine wave profile.

fibreglass insulation

View from Regent's Canal.

Elevational view.

Looking back from the 1990s to this London block of flats of the 1960s, it is hard to realize that it was seen, at the time of its birth, as such a pioneering venture. In structural and planning terms it broke new ground. It was the first residential building in the UK to be built with a central core, which challenged the building regulations and at the same time freed up the plans, allowing both flexibility and spatial ingenuity.

The building was first of all something of a political triumph; the architects negotiated a way through the maze of housing bureaucracy to create a situation that allowed a housing association to build a block of flats in central London. Secondly, the scheme represented an aesthetic challenge to the planning authorities, not just because the site next to Regent's Park was a sensitive one, but also because the architecture itself was certainly seen as trail-blazing.

On the political front, it was necessary for the Mercury Housing Society to both raise the funds – one-third of the cost of building from the government via the Housing Corporation and two-thirds from a building society (in this case, the imaginative leap was taken by the Cheltenham and Gloucester) – and to gain approval of the scheme from the planning authorities. The residents all shared in the ownership of the building, as did Nick Grimshaw himself who lived there for six years with his young family. Along with the other co-owners, he participated in the management of the building he had designed. This gave him an on-site understanding of his own building, as well as an opportunity to hear the views of the other occupiers at first hand. The flats turned out to be something of a seedbed for a whole range of talents – people who are now leading property

Apartments, 125 Park Road

Living room of a two-
bedroom flat on the north
side of the building.

Living room of an L-shaped
flat on the seventh floor
which occupies the south and
west sides of the building.

developers, designers, photographers and architects
chose these innovative flats to start their London
working lives.

The negotiations with the Housing Corporation
centred on the principle, 'the maximum amount of
accommodation for the minimum cost'. This was
achieved by designing some 40 flats gathered around
the central core, each having flexible plans by virtue of
the extensive perimeter glazing and lack of structure
between the core and the external walls. In cost terms,
the space was achieved without the usual 'developer's
costs': some valuers estimated at the time that it was
possible to offer these flats to the co-owners for some
50% less than full market price. Cost restraint meant
that this had to be a 'no frills' building – no balconies, a
simple and repetitious envelope and a plan form that
repeated floor by floor. One thing the Housing
Corporation insisted upon was that the flats should be
built to Parker Morris standards – standards for houses
and flats which have now, since the avaricious 1980s,
been relaxed as they were seen as 'too generous'.

Potential purchasers of the flats were allowed the
luxury of selecting the layout of the actual apartments
within the square plan form of the whole building, and
were given an amazing amount of choice by the
architect – some 73 variations of plan were presented
to them. Planning requirements necessitated the
lowering of the height of the original scheme by
25 feet so that the block should not be visible from
Regent's Park, where 100 feet is the maximum
permissible height of buildings seen in conjunction
with the Nash terraces.

The studio living room of Nick
Grimshaw's own flat on the
tenth floor in the north-east
quadrant of the building.
This photograph, taken
in 1970, shows Nick
Grimshaw's wife Lavinia,
their daughter Chloë and
John Young's son Adam.
John Young (now a partner
of Richard Rogers) was also
a resident of the building.

Apartments, 125 Park Road

As well as being an exercise in planning virtuosity, the design of this block made several advances in cladding and lightweight construction. At the time, the sinusoidal cladding in high-grade aluminium was considered adventurous because it demonstrated certain advantages of an architectural 'lightness of being'. The major advantage of the chosen cladding material was that it simplified the design of the curved corners with their single-glazed fixed lights. The curved corners also gave the flats beautiful panoramic views, especially those overlooking the park.

With this building, the practice began to face the sort of technological and architectural problems that come about with the use of new and sometimes untried materials, fixtures and fittings. Special problems always arise in adventurous designs, and in this case there were some ingenious solutions to do with sound reduction and with the exact relation of mullions to party walls. The planners' decision that the original height of the building had to be changed created some design problems, but the overall result was an extremely successful building. There is a rich variety of flats and particularly exciting penthouses with their double-height glazed spaces and galleries. In cost terms the building was remarkable at the time, achieving the extraordinarily low price of under £6 per square foot. This figure means little today, but demonstrated then that intense collaboration between the architects, planners and engineers, and a very special group of clients, can provide the recipe for a really good residential building on an important London site.

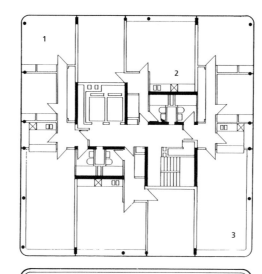

Typical floor plan
1 bedroom
2 kitchen
3 living room

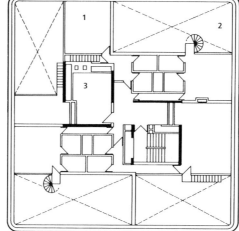

**Plan at penthouse
gallery level**
1 bedroom
2 double-height space
3 lift motor room

0   10m

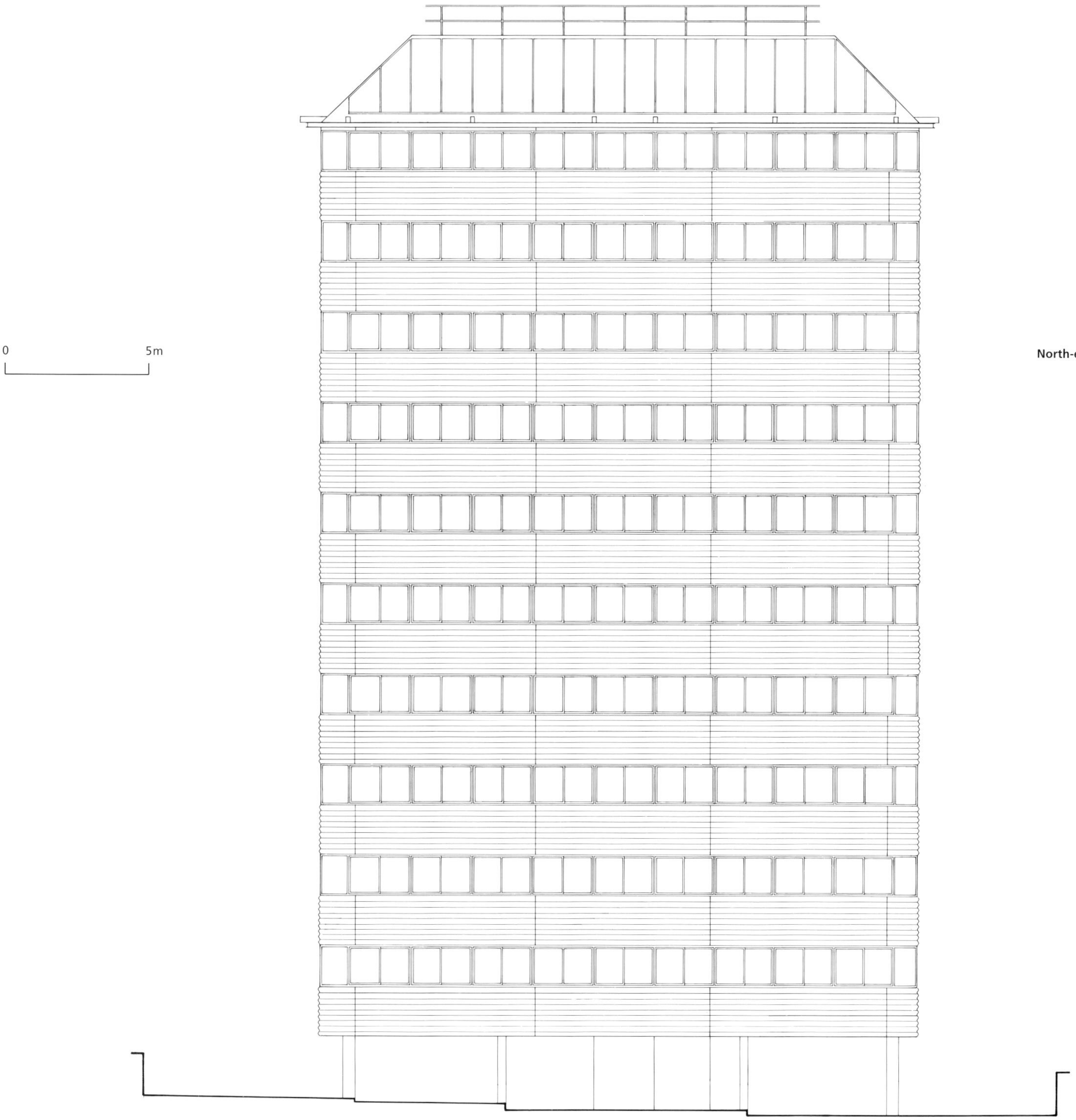

0   5m

North-east elevation   59

Apartments, 125 Park Road

Citroën Warehouse, Runnymede, 1972

'Citroën had acquired a marvellous riverside site. Our brief was to build a warehouse of maximum size and minimum cost, yet to make it as unobtrusive as possible. We did this by choosing a colour close to that of the muddy water of the Thames and by creating generous radii to "soften" the corners of the building. In order to reduce the scale, two housing units were positioned at the riverbank end of the building with boat stores underneath them. The apparent bulk of the building was further reduced by creating a continuous 2m-high grass bank around it, thus greatly helping the building to blend into the landscape.

'This was at the end of a period when acres of storage buildings had been constructed. Many of them were eyesores which were justified on the grounds of low cost. We set out to build not only at the same low cost, but also to create a structure which would be friendly to the environment and would stand the test of time.' **NG**

Riverside elevation.

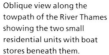

62

Oblique view along the
towpath of the River Thames
showing the two small
residential units with boat
stores beneath them.

Side elevation showing grass
bank which reduces the
apparent height of the
building.

The challenge that faced both the architect and the
developer on this Thameside site at Runnymede was a
difficult one: how can a large warehouse sit comfortably
and unobtrusively on a meadow on the side of the river,
while meeting all the sensitive environmental criteria?
The warehouse was a speculative venture by a securities
company that retained the freeholds of its investments.
Because the previous user of the site had been a paint
factory, there was a precedent for an industrial rather
than residential/domestic use of the site. Today, it looks
a curious scene with cottages and weekend retreats
crowding round the edges of the Gulliver-like
warehouse which arrived suddenly to share the
riverbank.

There were considerable planning problems because
of the historic nature of the immediate surroundings,
the scale of the new building and its visibility from the
Royal Air Force memorial which looks down from nearby
Egham Hill. The Royal Fine Art Commission looked at
the plans, as did the Council for the Preservation of
Rural England and the War Graves Commission. Their
advice was absorbed into the design to make it even
more well-mannered and self-effacing. Carefully chosen
colours for the cladding and roof material – olive green
and bronze – help this large building to be absorbed
into its surroundings. Nothing could make it invisible,
but care in design and choice of colours have made it
more neighbourly to its semi-rural environment.

The brief from the developer was for a single-storey
storage unit, with a clear storage space of 47,011m^3, to
be built to a low budget. It was three factors – the need
for the lowest cost, the largest span and the lowest
overall roof height (because of the sensitive nature of

Early perspective sketch.

the site) – that created the parameters of the design. The architects were able to make a deal in that they bartered a low-profile building in exchange for maximum coverage of the site.

The building is big – 67m wide and 18 bays long, each bay being 6.28m. But it maintains a very low height of a uniform 7m, while it has an acquired dignity from the grassed plinth that is necessary for flood resistance. The south elevation has six sets of 8.1m x 5m galvanized and painted folding doors, which slide back to reveal a cavernous loading bay. In the centre, three glass doors and a glazed staircase lead up to 930m² of open-plan offices. The offices are superimposed above the vigorous modelling of the loading bay doors.

The north elevation, fronting onto the river, attempts a more domestic scale. A pair of boxy residential units, glazed on three sides, jut out from the warehouse wall, each one offering two bedrooms, a sitting room, a kitchen and a bathroom, with a garage or a boat store below.

There is something of a conflict about this building that comes from the developer's wish for maximum flexible space and the planners' wish for something so unobtrusive that it should hardly appear in the landscape. To create the huge internal space, the architects and engineers adopted the structural solution of a variable cross-section propped steel cantilever. This structure comprises a central column with welded fillets and stiffeners at the top supporting a long I-section beam with a deeper middle section and a span of 33m. Each structural bay is made up of 66m variable cross-section steel beams, supported on central columns. The beams themselves are made from two standard

Top to bottom: front elevation; view across warehouse in full occupation as the central spare-parts store for Citroën cars.

Citroën Warehouse, Runnymede

South elevation

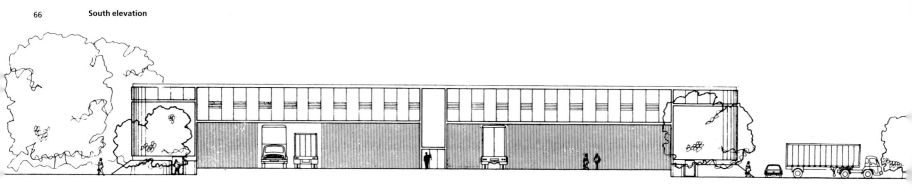

0   10m

**North elevation to the
River Thames**

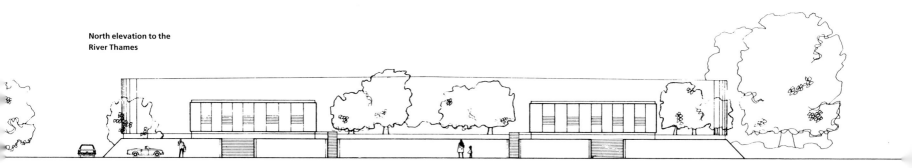

Architecture, Industry and Innovation

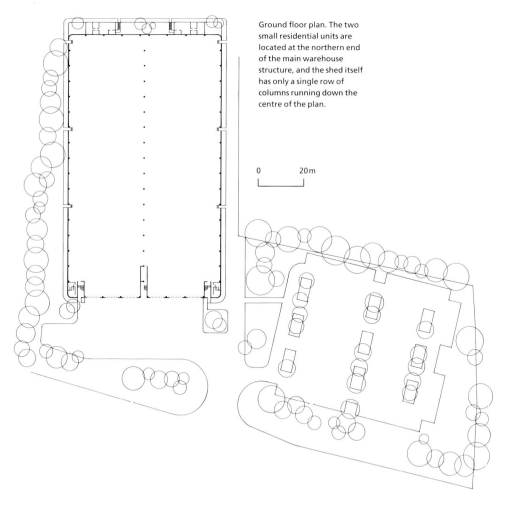

Ground floor plan. The two small residential units are located at the northern end of the main warehouse structure, and the shed itself has only a single row of columns running down the centre of the plan.

0   20m

universal sections measuring 915mm x 305mm and 685mm x 393mm, and weighing 88kg and 39kg respectively. Each was fabricated in three parts to make transportation and erection easier, and welded together on site with the aid of mobile scaffolding towers. The roof ridge lies over the central row of columns and conveniently provides the extra headroom needed to accommodate the thicker beam sections without increasing the internal floor-to-ceiling height of the warehouse.

The building has a ribbed metal cladding and the two projecting residential units, which relieve the extent of the long riverside elevation, are glazed. Simplicity and scale are the keynotes of this building – to cover 4,700m² in a single storey and remain relatively unobtrusive is no mean achievement.

Citroën has now leased the building as its main UK spare-parts depot and in retrospect even such luxury items as the power-floated concrete floor slab, designed to sustain applied loadings of up to 2,441kg to the square metre, appear to have paid off.

Citroën Warehouse, Runnymede

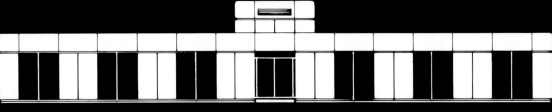

**Headquarters for Editions Van de Velde,
Tours, France, 1975**

'The building was a mixture of office, studio
and warehousing for Editions Van de Velde.
The site was a stone-walled cherry orchard
near the River Loire. The client wanted a low-
cost solution which reflected this mixture of
uses and offered maximum flexibility for the
activities to change. Allowance was even made
for a central courtyard. The simple steel frame
went up in a week and then, due to extreme
lack of cash brought about by the French
postal strike at the time, the client decided
to complete the building using his own staff.
This, therefore, became a genuine "hands-on"
project with the office handyman wielding
the Hilti-Gun.

'We tried to reflect the lush greenness of the
Loire Valley with green fibreglass panels and
glass the same colour as a Vouvray bottle. The
building has been through many changes and
is now occupied by a firm of accountants – thus
perhaps proving its value as a living organism
capable of reflecting change.' **NG**

The simple repetitive
structure was erected by an
English company in one week.

70   This elegant bright green pavilion in a cherry orchard on
the outskirts of Tours, France, was a pioneering example
of the flexible building, designed with future expansion
in mind. Van de Velde, a small family firm of music
publishers, saw an opportunity to cater for the growing
market in sheet music for use in French schools. Their
commission was for offices and a warehouse that could
expand around a courtyard. Music is itself a structural
discipline, and something of the harmony of an elegant
fugue is present in this small yet perfect pavilion.

     What can be seen in this project are many of the ideas
of a democratic workplace that are further developed in
larger schemes, like Herman Miller at Bath. The use of
completely interchangeable panels on the outside of the
building, and movable partitions on the inside, made
this something of a small-scale innovation. Everything
is on one floor and the client was able to make changes
to the internal arrangements after a while without any
difficulty. In many ways the cladding system was also
a prototype for the Herman Miller factory.

     This French building has considerable charm, sitting
in the orchard close to an old house. As many trees as
possible were saved and they considerably enhance
the views from the full-length windows. The office
furniture is by Herman Miller and all the lighting and
servicing is flexible.

Construction proceeds with
the client and members of the
office all lending a hand.

An early installation of
Herman Miller furniture.
This was serviced by a simple
overhead duct.

Elevational view showing the
interchangeable grp, glass
and louvre panels.

Previous page
Nick Grimshaw during a site
visit to Tours in 1974.

Headquarters for Editions Van de Velde

Plan of the whole building in
use as offices with the
warehouse built elsewhere.

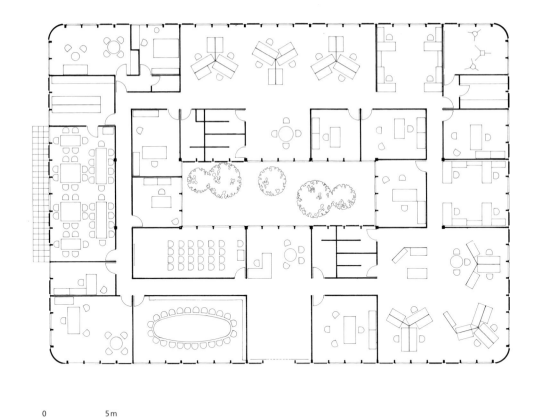

0   5m

72

Plan showing intermediate
use of the building with part
of the space used for
warehousing.

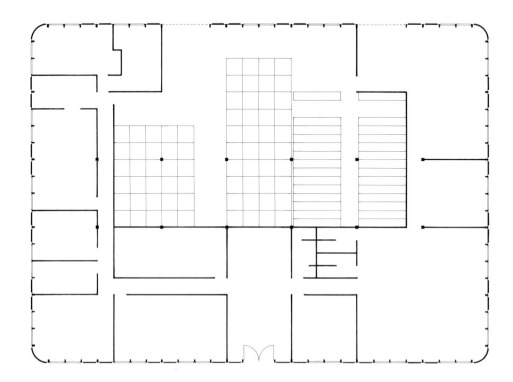

Often flexibility means that a client does not know exactly what he wants, but in this case the brief was clear and almost philosophical in its decision to create a place of work that would be efficient and also illuminate the lives of the employees by a fair distribution of space and a visual clarity that reflected the functional order. At the time this building was speedily being erected, the majority of architects working to this sort of commission were designing inflexible brick boxes around a portal frame with the inevitable bronze glass windows. The Grimshaw solution, which was to be much imitated, brought a shaft of intelligent light and a robust efficiency to the small business premises in a manner that was quietly revolutionary.

East elevation

0   5m

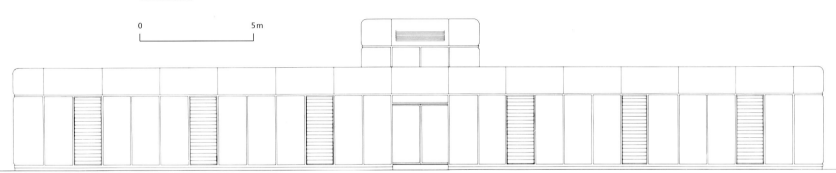

Headquarters for Editions Van de Velde

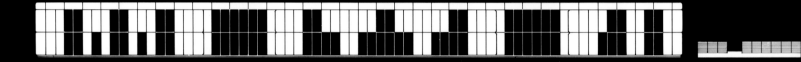

Factory for Herman Miller, Bath, 1976

'We had a fabulous riverside site in Bath; the
client was a household name in the world of
architecture; the brief was so short it was
practically a poem. Philosophically, the client
was almost ahead of us in terms of his concepts
of quality, flexibility and change; after all,
he had developed one of the first open-plan
office systems, "Action Office". Because of
the empathy with the client, the basic design
concept was agreed at break-neck speed.

   'There then began a meticulous period of
development to ensure that the details
really did match the concept. There was no
compromise. Solid panels can be changed for
glazed units, doors can be moved, even the
positions of the recessed courtyards can be
changed. In the end, I think we created a
building which was not only highly functional
from the manufacturing point of view, but
which offered a working environment far
in advance of its time.' **NG**

Previous page
Cross sections through
a sample grp panel for the
Herman Miller factory.

Left: distant view of the
factory showing how it 'fitted
in' with the scale and grain
of the city.

View of the factory on the
River Avon at Bath shortly
after its completion in 1975.

76 The combination of a fine site on the bank of the River
Avon near Bath and an excellent client with a reputation
for high quality design, were the right ingredients for
the architects to produce a remarkable building. The
brief for the new factory was prepared with great care
by Max de Pree, the managing director of Herman
Miller. It is an almost poetic series of statements:

Early model views showing
how all the services were
located so that they were on
separate grids to the
structure.

It is our goal to create an environment that:
Encourages an open community and fortuitous
*   encounter*
Welcomes all
Is kind to the user
Changes with grace
Is person-scaled
Is subservient to human activity
Forgives mistakes in planning
Enables this community (in the sense that an
*   environment can) to continually reach toward*
*   its potential*
Is a contribution to the landscape as an aesthetic
*   and human value*
Meets the needs we can perceive
Is open to surprise
Is comfortable with conflict
Has flexibility, is non-precious and non-monumental.

In our planning we should know that:
Our needs will change
The scale of the operation will change
Things about us will change
We will change.

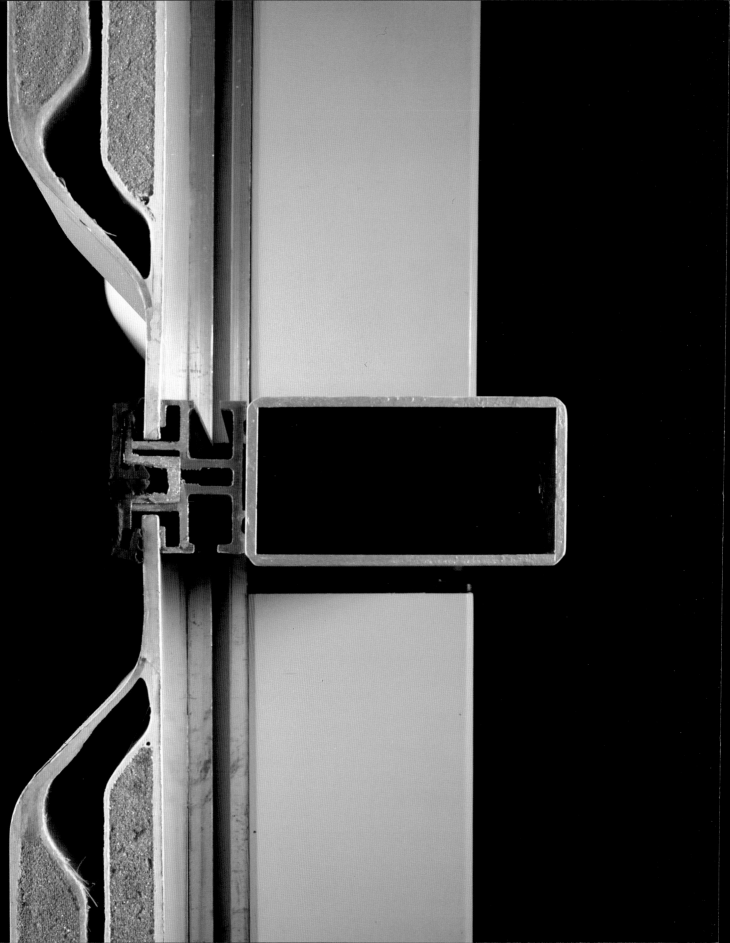

Nick Grimshaw checking a
prototype grp panel for
flatness.

Cross section of the
cladding system.

Nick Grimshaw's explanatory
sketch of the panel system for
the factory.

The brief went on to be more specific, to be more than a statement of expectations, and to list the criteria that were felt to be necessary for the well-being of the workforce and the necessity for flexibility of use.

It is often said that a good building can only be produced by the combination of a good client and the right architect, and in the case of Herman Miller the 'chemistry' between Max de Pree and Nick Grimshaw was so good that a harmonious result became almost inevitable. The striking similarity between the design of Herman Miller's elegant furniture and the neat resolution of the architecture is the most rewarding aspect of the Bath building. It is clear that the architect and the client learned a great deal from each other. The architect learned from the skilled production process that was fuelled by the constant infusion of good design methodology. The client learned the value of the imposition of a simplified architectural order and the application of an almost ruthless concern for structural integrity.

The client's demand for flexibility naturally led to a large span structure, which is a simple primary and secondary beam system with columns on a 10m x 20m grid. Only two rows of nine columns interrupt the 6m-high internal space. The cladding system, which was to become something of a trademark for a number of Grimshaw buildings, is a series of glass-reinforced polyesterpanels (grp) which are completely demountable.

The cladding frame of hollow steel section tubes span the height of the building to its primary beams, and spacing rails, located at the top, bottom and middle, span between the verticals of the cladding frame to provide additional support for the panels. The neoprene

4 Skin
G.R.P. panel.

Steel R.H.S as structural back-up.

"Top hat" extrusion to locate panel

Neoprene Gaskets.

Base Extrusion

Factory for Herman Miller, Bath

Three faces out of four of the building's elevations face public spaces. Here local schoolchildren happily race home past the building.

Axonometric showing how a panel is held in place using an aluminium extrusion which is screwed into position. A neoprene ring gasket then provides a weathering seal.

Sequence showing maintenance personnel removing a grp panel.

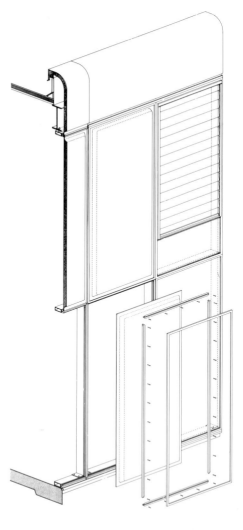

Architecture, Industry and Innovation

Oblique view showing the courtyard spaces and external seating for the workforce.

gasket system is fitted precisely into the steel sections.

Both the panels and their sophisticated support and gasketry system attain a quality seldom found in fibreglass panel detailing. The architects had a continuous dialogue with the manufacturers of both systems in order to achieve the level of finish they did. Grimshaw was exploring the possibility of using a system of aluminium panels. However, the fibreglass panels were considerably less expensive to model than developing a new system in aluminium at this scale.

Herman Miller's final industrial processes were not decided until well into the design development, so the building had to allow for sufficient height for palletized storage and a load-bearing capacity for heavy industrial equipment. Although the arrangement of glazing and panels seemed very formal, it has gradually changed with use. Already several doors have been moved from one part of the building to another – solid units, glazed units, louvres and doors can readily be interchanged and moved using unskilled labour.

This was characterized as the 'Action Factory', which seems appropriate since Herman Miller's Action Office furniture was produced there. The building provides 5,850m² of manufacturing space and initially accommodated 40 workers.

Nick Grimshaw with client Max de Pree fitting the last neoprene gasket to the building at its official opening in 1975.

The workforce at the official opening of the factory.

Factory for Herman Miller, Bath

View of the river from the working areas of the building.

Good quality lighting was needed at the factory so that materials could be colour-matched.

Other special features of this building include the primary servicing systems such as gas, electricity, water, compressed air and sprinkler systems; all of them can be reached by catwalks thus allowing for maintenance without any disturbance to the manufacturing process. A mobile lavatory unit can be moved to any of 16 positions in the building if necessary. The siting on the bank of the river encouraged the provision of open spaces – some of them created from indents in the facade allowing semi-sheltered courtyards with fixed furniture. All of the site is turfed and mature willows give a sense of relaxation and naturalness to the whole environment. The carefully chosen cream colour of the panels is not a random choice, but responds to the planners' wish for new buildings in Bath to relate to the predominant colour of the city's stone.

This building needs to be seen alongside some of its British counterparts. The Inmos factory in Wales by Richard Rogers (1982) and the earlier Reliance Controls factory by Team 4 (1966) are both in complete contrast to the simplicity of Herman Miller. Typically windowless working environments and, in the case of Inmos, elaborate external structural elements reflect a more aggressive high-tech approach to the problem of the design of the workplace. Herman Miller in Bath is a highly-unified expression of a brief that produced not simply cool and good architecture, but a harmonious workplace where managers and workers share the same space and the same high-quality environment.

Herman Miller evinces the simple, elegant architecture that results from a great deal of design development, research and skill. It was also inexpensive, comparable in price with the cheap, off-the-shelf systems that most industrial clients unfortunately still choose to erect.

View down one of the service catwalks giving access to control valves for all secondary services.

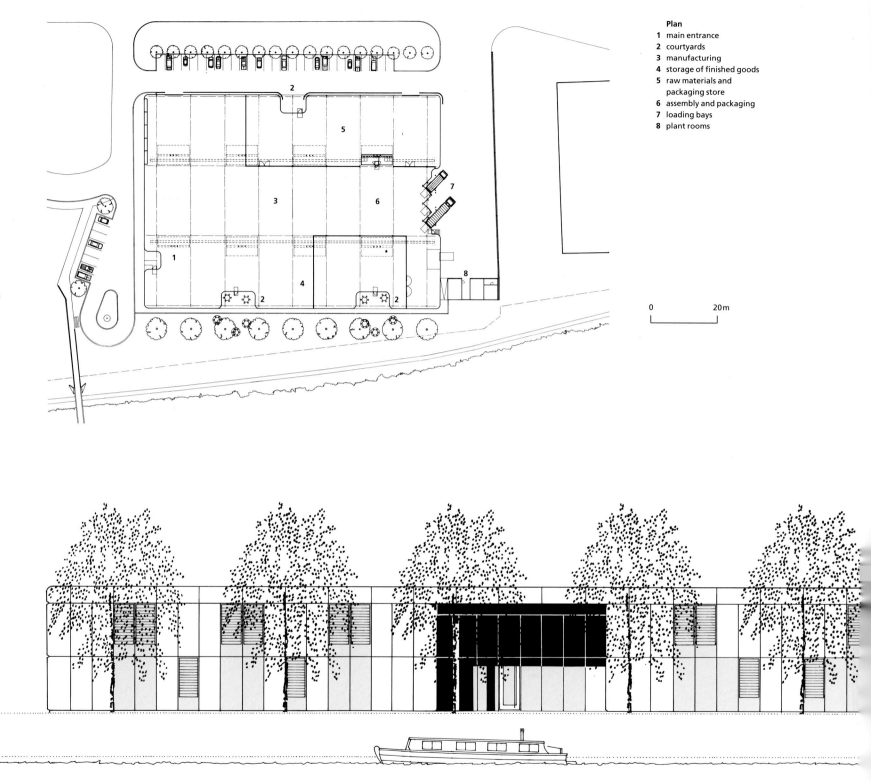

Plan
1 main entrance
2 courtyards
3 manufacturing
4 storage of finished goods
5 raw materials and
  packaging store
6 assembly and packaging
7 loading bays
8 plant rooms

0   20m

Architecture, Industry and Innovation

Elevation to River Avon

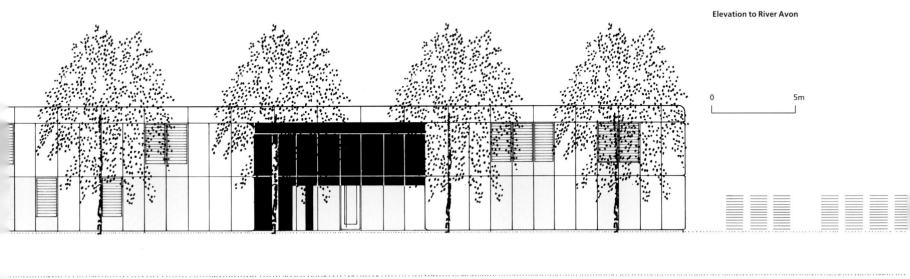

0   5m

Factory for Herman Miller, Bath

Advanced Factory Units, Winwick Quay, Warrington, 1978

'We never really knew whether the word "advanced" meant technologically advanced or if it referred to the fact that the buildings were the first on a new and difficult site – a sort of "advance guard".

'The chief architect of the New Town, who had a creative view on life, had seen the Herman Miller factory and felt that the concept of flexibility could be applied equally well to a number of small users as to one large user. He had a very unfriendly site – a former refuse tip – and he was determined to start off this new industrial area with an exciting building.

'We created a single "umbrella" roof which had the capability to shelter up to 25 different users, from very small high-tech manufacturers to large warehouse users. The whole system worked on 6mm-thick solid or glass panels which were interchangeable, as were the front doors and loading doors; even the stainless steel toilet modules could easily be moved by fork-lift truck and banked up in different arrangements.' **NG**

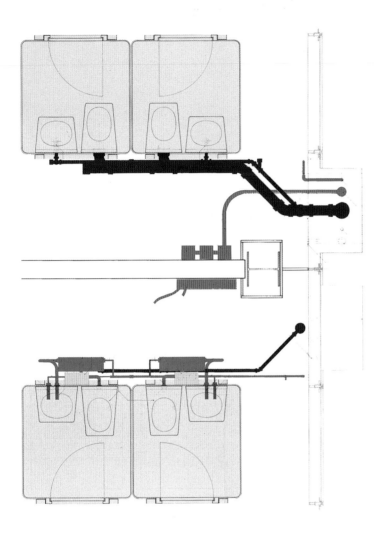

Left: back elevation of the
stainless steel lavatory modules
showing how the pallet-sized
units can be positioned using
a fork-lift truck.

The root of these industrial units was a feasibility study
carried out by the architects with the Development
Corporation of the newly expanded town of
Warrington. The requirement for the town was a new
kind of flexible, lettable unit that did not have the
drawbacks of so many portal frame buildings or cheap
speculative industrial sheds that frequently did not fulfil
their brief. The site, Winwick Quay, had been zoned for
industrial use being close to a motorway and having
been subjected to both mining subsidence and tipping.

The brief for the scheme was to provide as much
space as possible within a limited budget. The
Development Corporation and the architects, however,
saw the need to escape from the kind of inertia that so
easily produces a routine working environment that may
be cheap but does not, in fact, represent good value for
money. As has been proved before, inflexibility in
industrial buildings means difficulty in letting, which in
turn can often lead to premature demolition.

The solution lay in both the site layout and the
architectural design of the kit of parts that comprises
the architecture. The decision to design a perimeter
service ring for the whole building makes it possible
to alter the internal layout to suit the differing needs
of a variety of occupants; even lavatories can be
'plugged in' wherever they are needed. The uses vary
from warehousing to light industry and offices. These
mixed uses created the need for high ceilings, 6m to the
secondary beam; the flat roof was decided upon to
allow more flexible internal divisions. All the units were
grouped together under one umbrella roof covering
some 8,000m², with all-round accessibility. The building
is identical on each elevation; as the architects put it,

Bird's-eye view of one of the
stainless steel lavatory
modules.

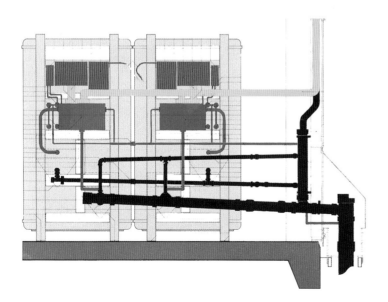

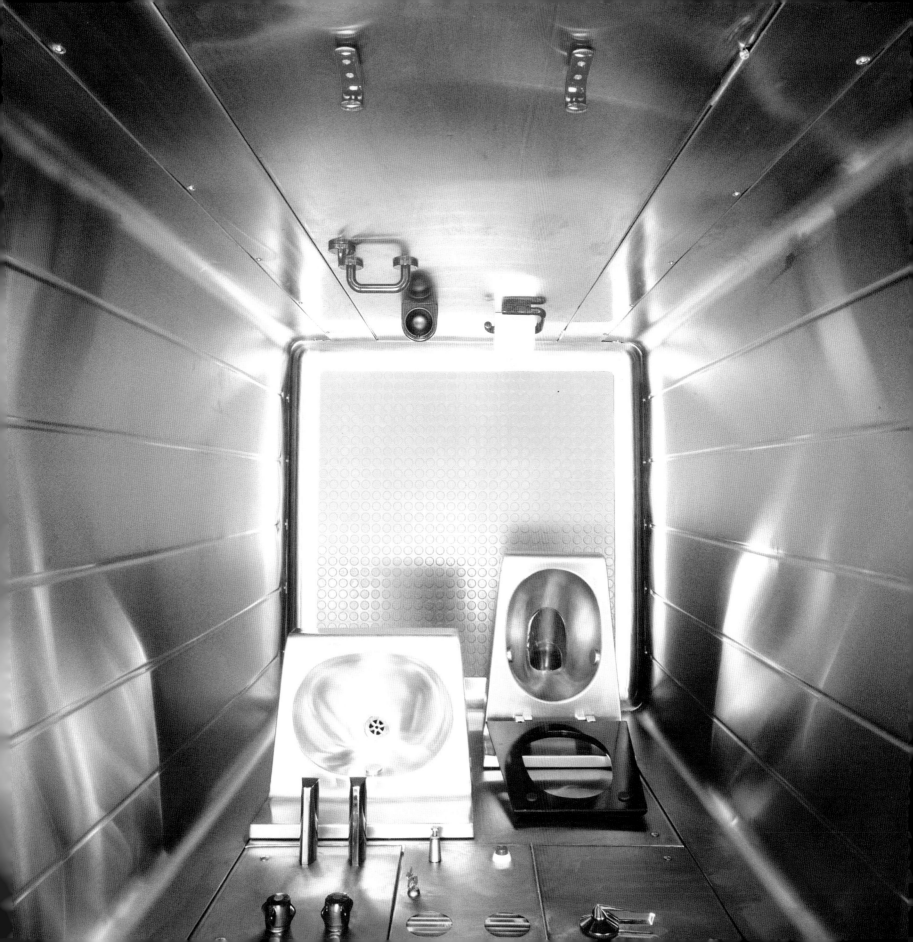

**Specially-designed
stainless steel
wc modules**
1 plan
2 front elevation
3 internal elevation
4 rear elevation
5 section
6 side elevation

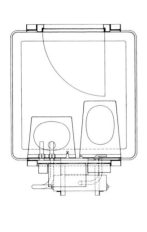

1

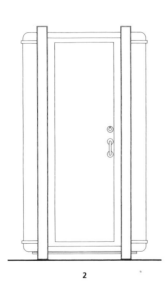

2

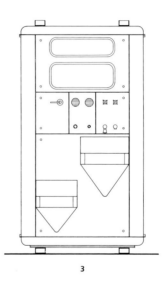

3

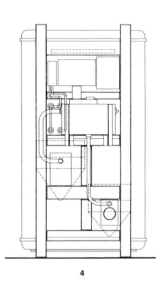

4

East elevation

0   10m

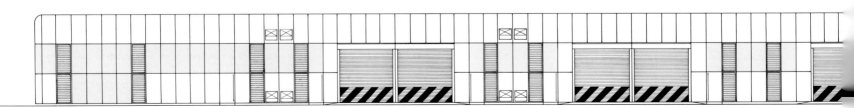

Architecture, Industry and Innovation

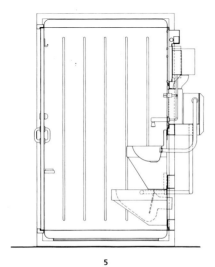

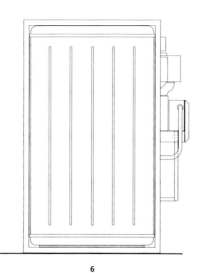

5   6

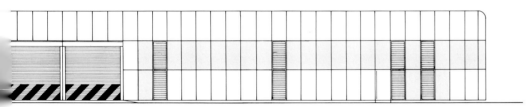

'there are no backs – only fronts', and the structure has been kept as simple as possible – based upon a grid of 10m x 17.5m with the primary beams at 10m centres. The cladding is a vertical mullion system accommodating a series of panels, glazed units, louvred units and access doors, all of the same 2.4m x 1.25m module. The Alucobond cladding panels are formed from coated aluminium on the exterior with a polyethylene core and mill-finished aluminium on the interior. The glass, louvres and plain panels are interchangeable. The four top corners of the building, which incorporate double curvatures, could not be formed in Alucobond and these were specially fabricated from grp. A lattice truss was introduced at a height of 4.8m around the perimeter allowing for roller shutter doors to be installed at any point.

Considerable work was done with the manufacturers to achieve the required quality and flexibility of the 'exterior kit of parts'. Doors, windows, rolling shutters, louvres, service hoods and the actual aluminium, Alucobond wall panels all had to be interchangeable. This was successfully achieved and the overall smoothness of the exterior is a tribute to the care that went into the design of the individual parts. The fully fitted out stainless steel lavatory cubicles of prefabricated modular design, which were small masterpieces of industrial design, were an impressive innovation at the time.

Warrington clearly demonstrated that it is possible to design simple industrial buildings to a very high standard at a reasonable price. It was described at the time by Peter Murray in the *RIBA Journal* as, 'a shining example of what can be done by careful design'.

Advanced Factory Units, Winwick Quay

Headquarters for BMW, Bracknell, 1980

'At the time, BMW seemed to have a strangely unromantic view of themselves. They were proud of the fact that their cars had a dash-board team, a front-end team and a team designing the "rear-end cluster", but no overall designer. Gradual evolution was the thing and the flourish of an overall concept was not for them.

'They had a similar attitude to architecture; in fact they chose a builder to put up their new UK headquarters. Fortunately for us the builder was Wiltshier who had built the Herman Miller factory a few years before. Our first and only "design and build" job was therefore born.

'The whole process from initial design concept to moving-in day took only 15 months. The steelwork programme was so fast we had to use two contractors in parallel. The chairman of BMW was delighted. He said "this would not have been possible in Germany". A compliment indeed.' **NG**

Previous page
Detail showing the continuous grp louvre band which was incorporated in the cladding. This allowed ventilation intakes and extracts to occur anywhere around the building's perimeter.

Site plan showing the two courtyards in the training centre which separates the office building from the warehouse.

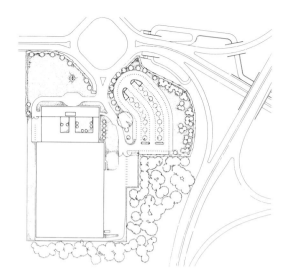

View of the building at dusk.

Detailed view illustrating
how the same cladding
system was used for
both the office and the
warehouse.

Cross section through the
four-storey office block.

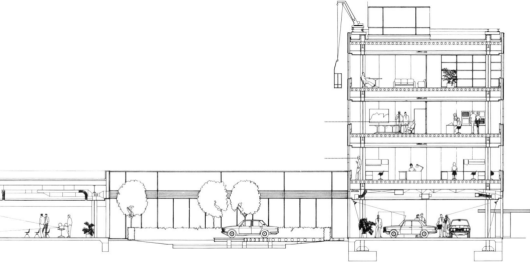

The pedigree of the BMW building owes a lot to its
forebear, the Herman Miller factory in Bath. The main
contractor for that building, Wiltshier, was asked by
BMW to find a site and an architect for its new parts
distribution centre and UK headquarters. Like many
other companies at that time, BMW chose the 'design
and build' method for this project – all the consultants
being selected by the main contractor.

BMW cars are known for the integrity of their
engineering and this was also to be a factor in the
design of their UK headquarters. The brief was for
10,200m² of warehousing with a clear racking height of
6.8m, a 1,750m² training centre and 4,000m² of offices,
amenities and showrooms. The offices overlook two
courtyards which are landscaped.

A key element of the brief was speed of erection
because the company was closing all its existing
buildings throughout the UK and spare parts from a
variety of places were to converge simultaneously on
Bracknell on 1 January 1980. To achieve the expediency
required for the company to meet its trading
programme, an architectural solution was devised that
was simple and single-minded.

The paramount factor that allowed for a large
amount of off-site prefabrication was the design of the
cladding system, which was used for the whole
development. This consisted of aluminium face sections
and neoprene zipper gaskets on a uniform 5m x 1.5m
modular support system. A white pre-finished
aluminium panel by Alucobond was used which
consisted of two aluminium skins with a dense
polyethylene core. At an intermediate level around the
building, a 500mm louvre panel allows the services to

Headquarters for BMW

View of the ground floor
showroom.

be accommodated as desired with no puncturing of the
building skin. There are no ducts, wires or pipes on the
outside of the building. The roof is detailed without
falls, the natural deflection being used to direct
rainwater to the outlets located at the midspan points.

To meet the fast-track programme, steel was adopted
as the simple, highly repetitive structure and for the
staircases. Sizes of beams and columns were chosen
carefully to limit the number of conditions; one basic
column and two beam sizes for the warehouse and link
building, and one beam and one column size for the
offices. The office block is a four-storey single-bay portal
frame with a span of 10m and a cantilever of 1.25m.
The offices have curved corner glazing and can be open
plan or cellular.

The three distinctive types of user – office, warehouse
and showroom – are all united by the common use of
materials and the elegance of the detail. The project was
completed in record time – a mere 17 months from
inception to occupation – due to the forethought that
had devised a structure and panel system that was easily
fabricated off site and rapidly erected.

This BMW scheme demonstrates clearly the early
Grimshaw methodology. This can be summarized as the
development of a simple structural grid that allows for a
dry envelope cladding system, thus enabling a speedy
start on site. In this case construction work started
within a few weeks of the architect securing the job and
the structural steel work accounted for about half of the
construction time. There is a simplicity and elegance
about this curvaceous clad building that won the
support of the planners and successfully reflected the
image of the company.

Oblique view which illustrates
the design intention of
integrating the office training
centre and warehouse using
the same cladding system.

Sections through the office
wall (left) and warehouse
wall showing their respective
cladding and servicing
arrangements. The modular
cladding panels can be varied
to suit the changing plan
condition.

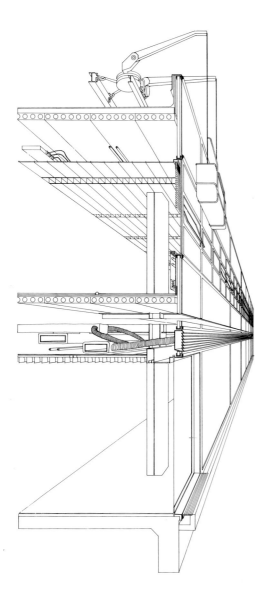
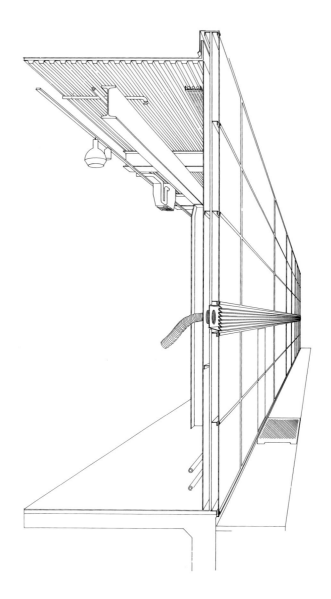

East elevation

0   20 m

Plan
1 showroom
2 workshop
3 courtyards
4 training centre
5 ancillary offices
   for warehouse
6 warehouse
7 loading bays

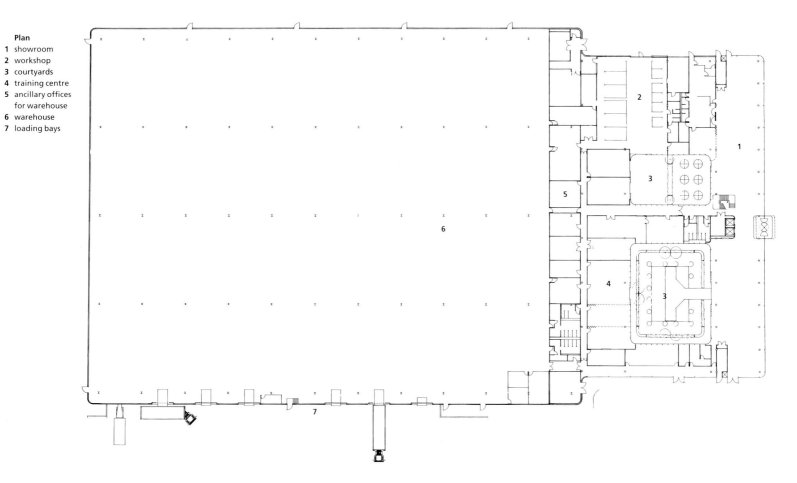

Headquarters for BMW

**Factory Units, Queen's Drive,
Nottingham, 1980**

'This was a time when rents were low and
industrial space was being erected by the acre.
On this long strip of land, sandwiched
between the railway tracks and a main road,
we had to achieve a very high site coverage
at a low cost, and yet erect buildings of
architectural merit.

   'The buildings could not have been more
straightforward with a simple steel structure
and blockwork party walls. However, our
achievement was in the perspective view
where bright green fibreglass service towers
broke up the elevation and allowed the
maximum amount of usable space to be
created inside the buildings.

   'This was a minimalist scheme but it
showed that even on the most difficult site
and with the lowest possible cost, the
application of "architecture" could improve
the quality of industrial buildings.' **NG**

Previous page
Oblique view of the facade
showing the service towers
which contained staircases
and lavatory units.

Elevational view showing
how the service towers were
used to articulate the 400m
long facade.

These units are a marriage of two key Grimshaw ideas:
the simple and flexible clad box and the service/
circulation tower – the pod meets the economical shed.
Service towers have played a role in Grimshaw's
thinking since his thesis days at the Architectural
Association; they were developed for the early student
hostel project as a natural way to update the services of
old London terraces. Here at Nottingham – where the
warehouse factory building at 260m is as long as the
Chrysler building in New York is high – the towers also
have an aesthetic role to punctuate the length of the
facades. The towers house the stairs and the lavatories
and they add cheerfulness with their bright green
colour, their domed tops and glossiness.

A series of steel-framed warehouse units varying from
346m^2 to 2,864m^2, are situated on a long, tight site
running north to south between a major road and the
railway. The two blocks are divided by a service road
with forecourts and parking bays enlivened by trees and
beds of periwinkle. The sheds are clad with 5m-long
galvanized horizontal sheeting which is fixed to the
stanchions with self-drilling, self-tapping screws capped
with water-protective plastic heads. The towers are clad
in panels which incorporate two layers of glass

Aerial view.

107

Oblique view showing how important the brightly coloured service towers were in enlivening the urban context.

Cross section of service tower showing reception area at ground level, lavatory unit at intermediate level, and access to first floor offices at the top.

108

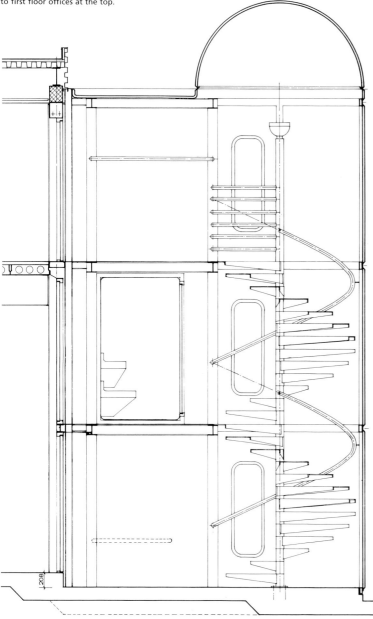

208

reinforced polyester (grp) with a layer of polyurethane foam between, and are screwed to a steel structure like the panels on the sheds. The big roller doors are standard industrial items; windows are of anodized aluminium and were specially fabricated by shipwrights. The roof is made up of chippings on high tensile roofing felt on top of insulation which is supported by troughed metal decking. Roof drainage takes advantage of the deflection in the rectilinear frame and drainage outlets are located at the points of greatest sag.

It is the contextual question which this building answers so well. It rejuvenated a railway-side location which was a typical dismal stretch of industrial wasteland. It created a new scale of industrial landscape, but its careful composition prevented gigantism from overwhelming the site; and, instead, it offers a transforming beacon for a dismal area.

Plans of the service towers
at ground, intermediate and
first floor levels.

0   20m

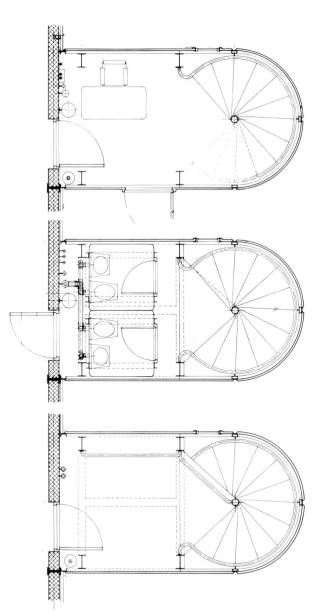

View at the top of the spiral
staircase where uplighting
dramatically highlights the
shape of the grp dome.

Factory Units, Queen's Drive, Nottingham

Aerial perspective by Paul
Burrows.

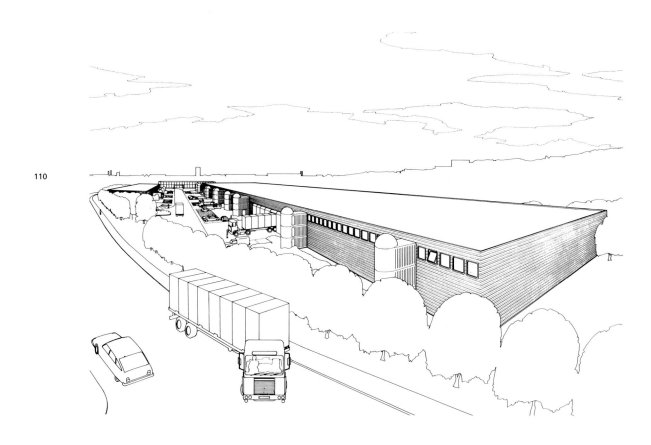

South elevation

0   20m

The project architect
discovered that the building's
plan was similar to the cross
section of the Chrysler
Building, and laid out the car
park at the end of the site to
represent the top of that
famous New York skyscraper.

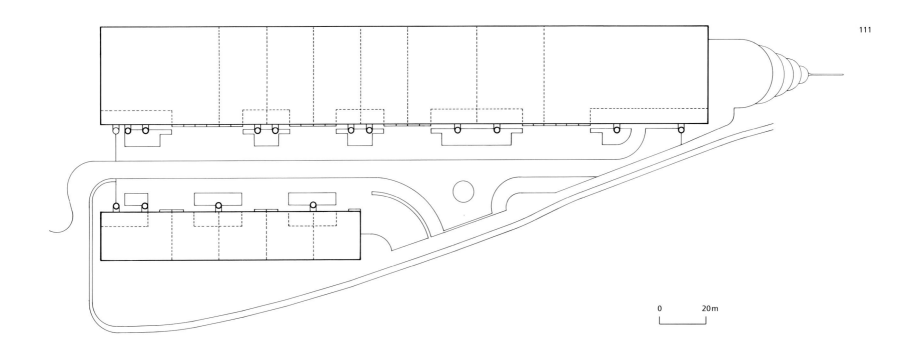

0   20m

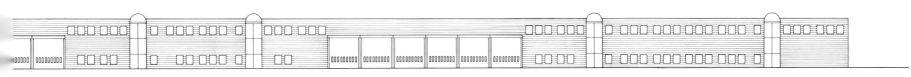

Factory Units, Queen's Drive, Nottingham

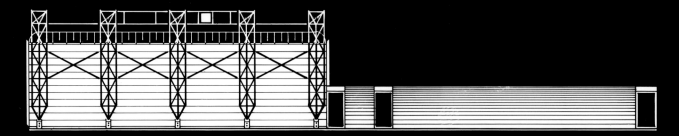

Sports Hall for IBM, Winchester, 1980

'The brief was for a low-cost air-conditioned
enclosure for three badminton courts.
However, other ball games would also be
played, many of which involved playing off
the walls. No internal obstructions could
therefore be allowed. We opted for a totally
external structure with flat insulated industrial
panels which formed both the internal and
the external skin. Then came the problem of
convincing the Winchester Planning
Committee.

   'They had established a reputation for
insisting that all buildings in their domain
should be in brick with slate roofs. They
were not in the mood to change their policy.

Oblique view of the
sports hall with the old cricket
pavilion in the background.

114

Before Nick Grimshaw was commissioned for this
building, IBM had converted a country house outside
Winchester in Hampshire as a training centre. They
then commissioned a certain number of new buildings,
including this sports hall facility for the staff as a part
of the IBM social club. Because of its proximity to the
existing pavilion, a simple link was provided and the
possibility for future extension formed a part of the plan.

The original house stands in a mature parkland
setting and this created both opportunities and
restraints. The building's visible external structural
framework appears to echo the branches and angular
geometry of winter trees. But at a functional level, as
the brief was for a hall to be used for badminton and
other indoor sports, large areas of wall were necessary,
and a space free of internal structural members had
many advantages.

Structurally the scheme is simple with five trussed
portal frames, spanning some 18m, creating the
external framework from which the roof is suspended.
The cladding of the main building is silver-finished
panels with blue curved grp panels at the corners which
help to reduce the apparent scale of the whole building.

The wall panels, 5,250mm long and 500mm high, are
simply 42mm thick industrial door panels, bolted at
each corner to cleats on the frame. There are no
cladding rails or secondary framing. Vertical joints
between panels are expressed as a 15mm gap into
which a neoprene gasket is inserted and the joint
caulked. The roof covering is of a PVC sheet material
with pre-formed upstands of rigid PVC which can be
joined to form a single waterproof covering.

The interior gives a great sense of openness with no

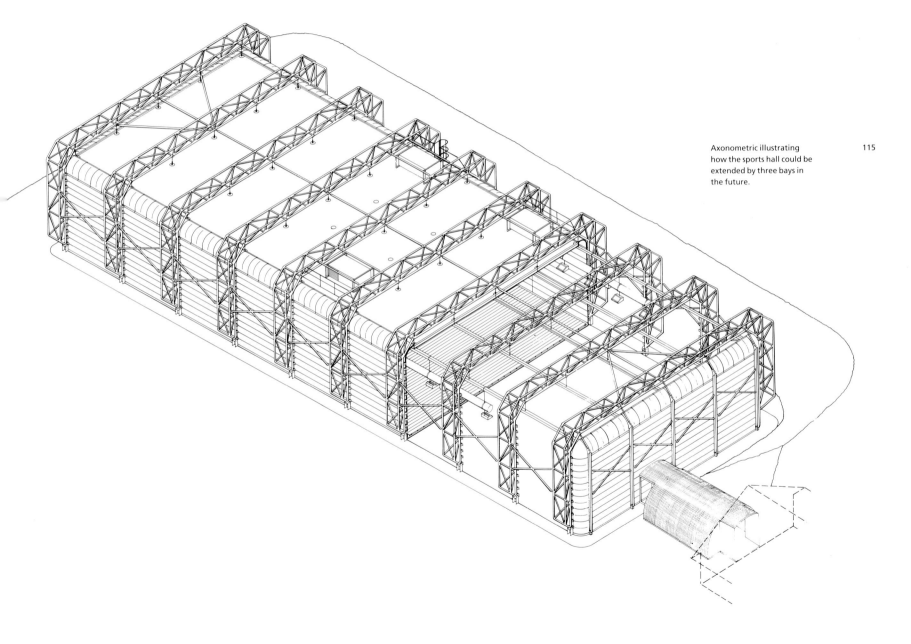

Axonometric illustrating
how the sports hall could be
extended by three bays in
the future.

Sports Hall for IBM

Standard industrial panels were fixed back to the main structure by specially fabricated steel T-brackets.

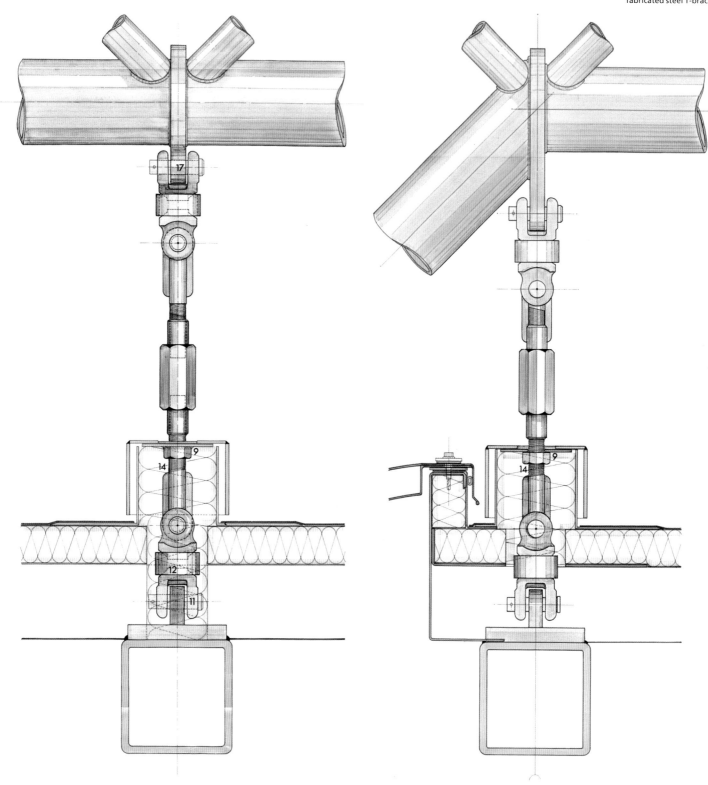

View of the sports hall. The completely flush interior was created by placing all the structure on the exterior of the building.

The sports hall in use for indoor football practice.

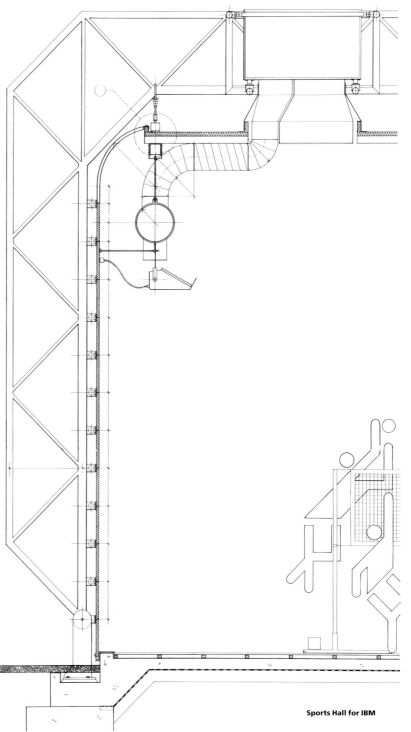

119

suspended ceilings and careful attention to the detailing of the visible services. The five main planes of the hall – the four walls and the roof – are articulated by a continuous slot that lets the light in, adding a floating dimension to an apparently solid structure. The link to the old pavilion has a more robust quality reading as a corrugated steel tunnel with a continuous skylight. Throughout this sports complex there is a sense of controlled energy in the design which is powerful in its clarity and vigour.

This sports hall could easily have been, what the architect calls, 'a sham Edwardian chapel'. In fact, it is Grimshaw's first ever job built without a post and beam structure. It represents an important stage in the practice's *œuvre* and the process that led to its exo-skeletal structure has informed many later Grimshaw schemes.

Sports Hall for IBM

Roof plan

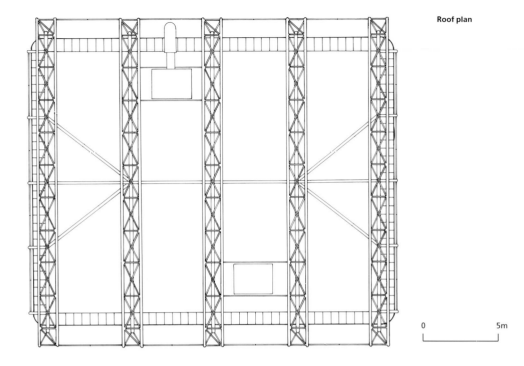

0   5m

Ground floor plan

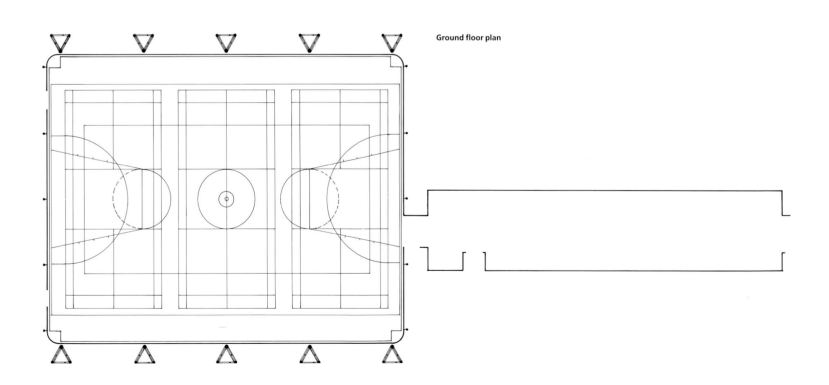

Architecture, Industry and Innovation

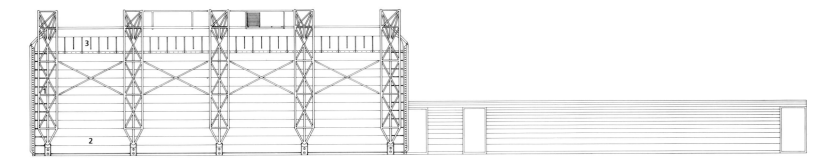

South elevation
1 trussed portal frame
2 steel-skinned composite
  sandwich panels
3 translucent double
  skinned grp panels giving
  glare-free light

**Furniture Factory for Vitra,
Weil-am-Rhein, Germany, 1981**

'I received an urgent telephone call from Rolf
Fehlbaum of Vitra; half their factory had
burned down and they only had enough
insurance to cover six months' loss
of production.

'At first we thought a cable-supported fabric
structure would provide the fastest solution,
but it turned out that cables for this span were
on six months' delivery! We therefore selected
a very neat pre-cast structural system and work
began on site within three weeks.

'The lining panels and insulation followed
the structure so that fit-out could proceed in
parallel with the cladding. We continued our
philosophy of using service towers, which
proceeded independently of the main
structure. Finally, we installed a gently curved
ceiling in the office area which was somehow
reminiscent of the snow-drifts outside.

'The first container lorry of furniture left
the factory exactly six months after our
telephone call – 15,000m² of factory had been
completed.' **NG**

Nick Grimshaw met Rolf Fehlbaum of the Vitra furniture business by chance in London when he was launching his newest chair design at the Institute of Contemporary Arts in 1980. A few months later Fehlbaum's Basle factory, where the Vitra range was manufactured, burned down and a new building was needed urgently. Fehlbaum was impressed by Grimshaw – especially by the Herman Miller factory – and sensed that he understood the furniture design and manufacturing process. He also felt that Grimshaw had a real feeling for industrial buildings and that he would be capable of finding a way of getting a new building up and running in the shortest possible time.

The Vitra company is more than just a furniture manufacturer – it is a family firm, and Fehlbaum's name is associated with a broad patronage of contemporary art, design and architecture. His early patronage of Grimshaw has been followed by commissions for many other major figures including Frank Gehry, who has

Above: east facade showing the service towers providing stairs and toilet facilities to the building.

Opposite: detail of the facade illustrating how curves were used to help the building blend into its surroundings.

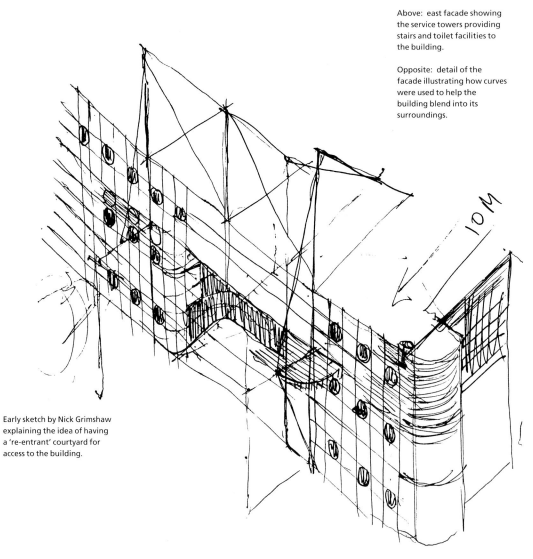

Previous page
Detailed view of the cladding. The large scale sinusoidal cladding at 150mm pitch used for the main facades contrasted with the 50mm profile cladding used for the service towers.

Early sketch by Nick Grimshaw explaining the idea of having a 're-entrant' courtyard for access to the building.

Architecture, Industry and Innovation

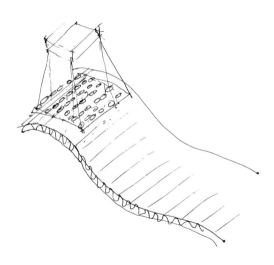

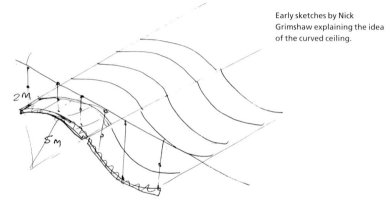

Early sketches by Nick Grimshaw explaining the idea of the curved ceiling.

Interior view showing how holes were provided in the pre-cast roof beams to allow the passage of air distribution ducts.

Interior view of the first floor showroom area. A standard suspended ceiling was used to create interest in the space by forming the suspension track into a sinusoidal curve.

designed a chair museum, and most recently Zaha Hadid and Tadao Ando. The Vitra site is in Germany, close to the Swiss border, and is served by the international airport at Basle.

The setting for the furniture factory and its ancillary buildings is almost rural, with wooded hills and distant mountains forming the backdrop to a maverick collection of recent buildings and sculptures. To meet the terms of Vitra's fire insurance policy, work on the new building had to be completed within six months. After originally considering a temporary solution of a tent-like suspended structure, it was decided that a permanent structure was possible within the time frame and although the design period may have been shorter than is ideal, the result does not reveal this.

All servicing and accommodation ancillary to the factory was housed in towers outside the building or at roof level to allow for a flexible production floor. The fast-track construction was assisted by the use of a standard pre-cast concrete frame that spanned 25m. A double-skin wall was put up in two stages so that production could begin as soon as the first layer of sheeting and insulation was in place.

The office and showroom interiors are quite different from the manufacturing space. One particular feature that marks this is the wave-form acoustic ceiling that adds drama to the offices, and especially to the showroom area where much of the Charles Eames range is elegantly displayed in a white, grey and black setting. As the *Architectural Review* said at the time, in 1983, 'it faithfully catches the spirit of the elemental architectural furniture the factory produces'.

Furniture Factory for Vitra

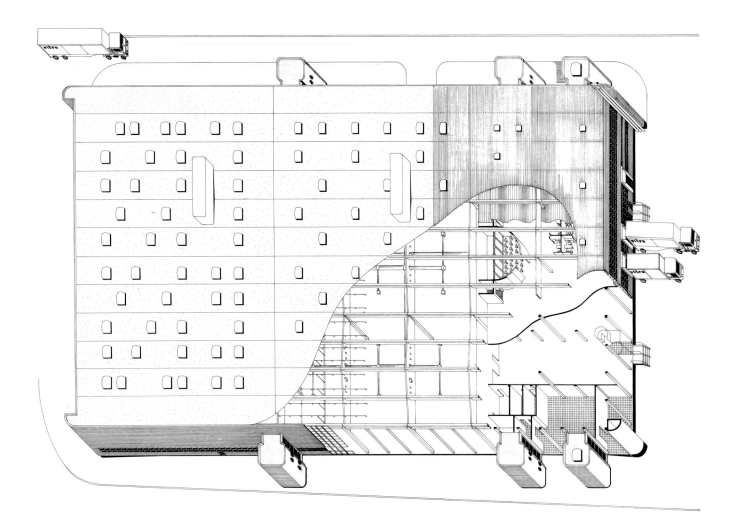

128

Axonometric sketch
illustrating arrangement of
loading bays, office areas,
industrial areas and
service towers.

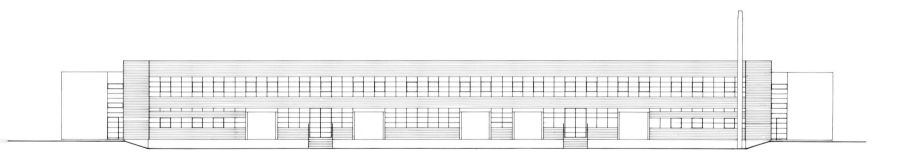

North-east elevation

0   10m

North-west elevation

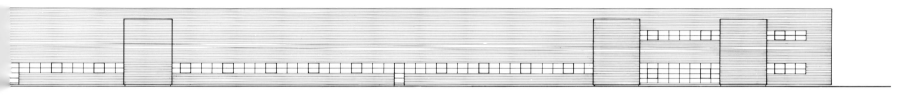

Furniture Factory for Vitra

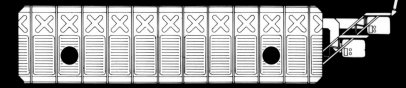

Wiltshire Radio Station,
Wootton Bassett, 1982

'At a time when many local radio stations
were being set up, our client won the
franchise for Wiltshire. They had bought
a 17th-century Cotswold rectory for their
offices, but knew it could not meet the highly
technical demands of recording studios.

'We put to them the idea of having
a "space ship" in their walled vegetable
garden and they responded with enthusiasm.
However the on-air date was an absolute
fix and to complete this complex and
technically intricate project in the time
allowed proved very difficult.

'In spite of bankruptcies, late deliveries,
components not fitting, bad weather and
every other possible disruption, the building
was completed by the on-air date. It was
rather poignant during our later site visits
to Chippenham to listen to the transmissions
from this tiny building that had caused us so
much stress.' **NG**

Oblique view.

Part elevation showing the grp cladding panels which were filled with sand to provide the necessary acoustic attenuation.

Detailed elevation of one of the building's grp panels.

A brief for six radio studios and a news reporters' room, situated under the flight path of an RAF training station and adjoining a listed manor house, is something of a challenge both acoustically and architecturally. The solution Grimshaw designed for Wiltshire Radio at Wootton Bassett shows that nothing is impossible. The building is really an acoustic box that makes no pretensions to be more than a functional building – albeit a handsome one. Apart from the sound studios and the news room, the building also contains a racks room for heavy equipment and a reception area, and the station's programmes are cabled from here to the Swindon area transmitters.

The studios form a box built of concrete blockwork which is then enclosed by a protective casing of acoustic material. The acoustic jacket was designed by the architects and it is formed from specially-designed grp panels. The pale grey panels are tall, thin boxes filled with sand. After they were fixed in place on 200mm x 100mm concrete-filled steel tube columns, the builders poured and vibrated the sand in from the top through circular hatches formed by standard gasketed marine fittings. Each panel or box has two of these hatches on the chamfered top, and another on the bottom for emptying should a panel need to be replaced. The sand

Previous page
View from one of the recording studios into the central corridor. Clearly visible are the various acoustic wall treatments which contributed to the broadcasting quality of the building.

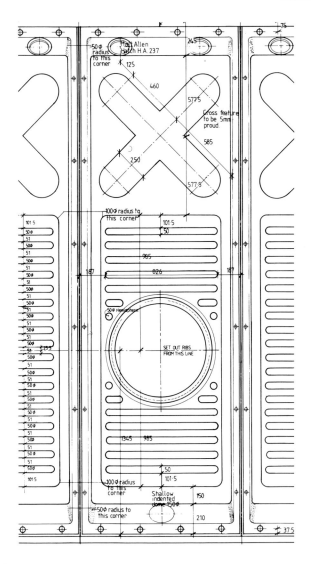

View down the central
circulation corridor.

'Porthole' which gives
a view out for broadcasters
in contrast to the totally
enclosed spaces with which
they are more usually
provided.

Detail of the aluminium
structure supporting the
glazed rooflights over the
reception area.

deadens the sound in exactly the same way as a stone
wall would. Rubber mattress foam on the studio walls in
various thicknesses is also an effective absorbent agent
of a whole range of sound frequencies. The corrugated
patterning on the panel surface is an integral stiffening
which increases their capacity to resist the pressure and
to stop panels bulging under the weight of the sand. A
specially-made neoprene extrusion seals the joints
between panels.

The central top-lit corridor has a sense of drama –
above its spartan white-painted blockwork walls, a
great river of services flows contained by two elegant
metal wiring trays. These trays carry all the electrics in
the corridor, including warning lights over each studio
door and the rows of low-energy fluorescent bulbs
attached to the outer edges of the trays. The only
internal colour is provided by the blue doors; and the
circular porthole windows in the studio doors echo the
larger circular windows that light the main studios and
give the outside of the building something of a capsule-
like appearance.

Grimshaw himself admits that this is an incredibly
simple building that deals directly with the technical
problems of sound absorption and noise isolation.
It was also built within a very tight budget. For such
a relatively modest building, it has an extraordinary
presence standing, as it does, in the garden of a modest
English village house.

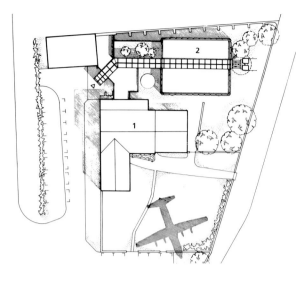

Site plan
1 Old Lyme House
2 Studio

Plan
1 Old Lyme House
2 entrance canopy
3 existing garage
4 reception
5 racks room
6 newsroom
7 courtyard
8 news
9 on air
10 talks
11 production studio
12 production control

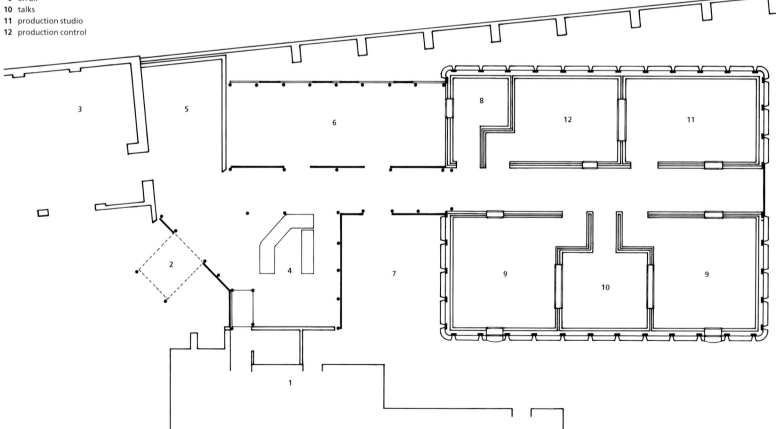

Architecture, Industry and Innovation

0   5m

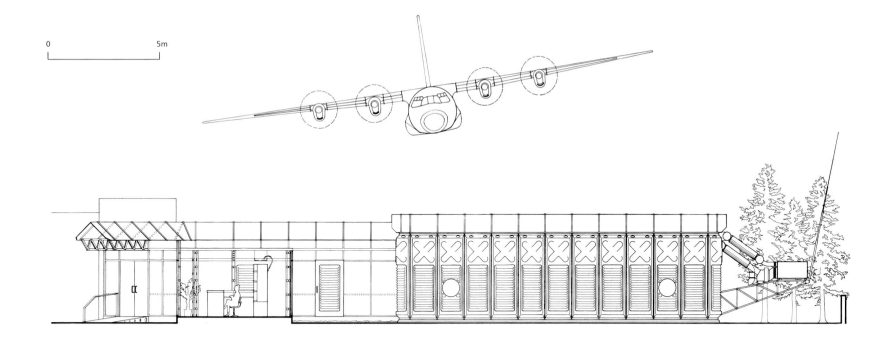

Wiltshire Radio Station

**Herman Miller Distribution Centre,
Chippenham, 1982**

'I remember having a family picnic on this site
and listening to the high-speed diesel trains
thundering past on the embankment and the
noise of the traffic on the busy main road. I felt
that any building in this setting would have to
fight hard to hold its own.

'With this opportunity of doing a second
building for Herman Miller, we wanted to
stick to the philosophy of a completely flexible
facade with interchangeable panels, windows
and doors. We succeeded in this in a more
sophisticated way than before by using thick
aluminium panels with perforated aluminium
acoustic panels inside and insulation between.
The whole facade was fixed to double
unistruts.

'I believe that with this project we probably
got closer to the genuine multi-use building
than ever before. It certainly could be used
for manufacturing, warehousing or offices.
However it would also make a fine retail
building and even possibly a sports centre or
an art gallery. The ultimate long-life loose-fit
building.' **NG**

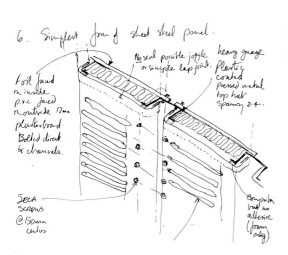

Initial sketch by Nick Grimshaw exploring a simple aluminium panel system for the building.

Right: aluminium panel being removed from the break press.

Opposite: a good 70% of the design time on this project was spent developing the cladding system, a true 'meccano kit' that allows the demountability of solid panels, windows, vents, doors, service hoods and external lights, not to mention loading bay doors.

142 The brief for this building for Herman Miller was for 6,970m² of warehouse space with an overall minimum height of 6.5m. Potential for expansion was needed to allow for the building to grow to up to three times its initial size. The client also wanted a large degree of flexibility – other potential uses besides warehousing included offices, manufacturing, paint spraying and staff canteens. The company wanted to continue and emulate the success of the entirely flexible premises at Bath designed by Grimshaw in 1976.

The site is on the outskirts of Chippenham between the heavily-used trunk road to Bath and the noisy, elevated main London–West Country railway line. In fact, the architect felt that the site was somewhat overpowered by these elements and could therefore accommodate a strong architectural statement. As in the earlier commission from the same company (see page 74), the driving force for the client side was Max de Pree. By 1982 he had become the President of Herman Miller; he retained his intense interest in the quality of design and the importance of design for the entire company. He wrote to the architect at the time:

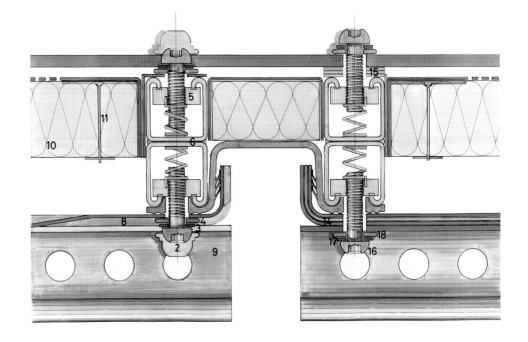

Page 139
Close-up view of cruxiform panel joint.

Previous pages 140–1
The 94-m long east elevation from the adjoining pasture.

Right: details showing how the back-to-back 'unistrut' system was able to support panels on both the inside and outside of the building.

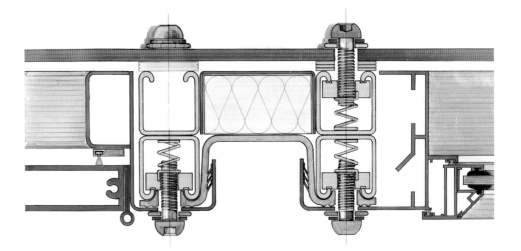

I am most grateful for the ways you have been able to integrate your own creative gifts into meeting the very special needs of Herman Miller. I do believe we're a very special company and a special client, but I also realise that doesn't make the job any easier. In many ways it just makes things more difficult. I respect greatly your talent and also your courage in making sure that our potential together is realised, as you have now done both on the Bath and Chippenham projects, rather than take the easier road of compromise.

With this exceptional backing there was never any chance of the client's reversion to the rural vernacular, and the opportunity was there for something of an architectural landmark. An early proposal had an expressed external structure, but this did not prove to be acceptable to the building's financial backers in the form of conservative pension fund managers.

North-east corner of the building from the landscaped staff rest area.

Nick Grimshaw's sketches of the lavatory pod. With this concept, all services that have nothing to do with the warehousing process are kept clear of the main slab.

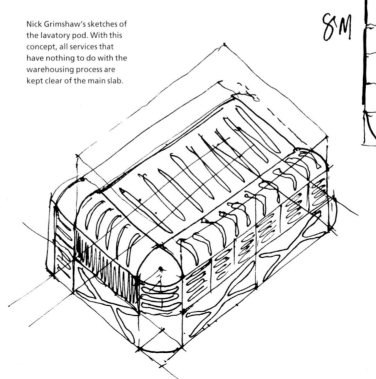

5M

8M

Left: the warehouse empty.

Right: the warehouse full.
Note the small office suite to
the right.

The built design gets much of its excitement, not from the structure, but from a strong emphasis on colour and the quality of the finished detail of the individual elements. The cladding panels were pressed aluminium and even more technically developed than those at Bath. They were easier to change around and the substitution of glazing panels for solid panels could be easily accomplished.

The structure is a simple one. A post and beam framework based upon a central span of 36m and two side spans of 28.8m. Together with the 6.5m clear internal height, this gives considerable racking flexibility. The circular steel plates cut from the beams' webs (reducing their weight) have been used ingeniously as fixed seats in the external relaxation area. The cladding is set out on a 2.4m x 1.2m grid and is conceived rather like the product that Herman Miller makes – the Action Office furniture range – a well-designed kit of interchangeable parts. The doors and windows, as well as the solid panels, can be fixed and unfixed and moved easily. Window glazing can also be readily changed. A simple neoprene gasket between the panels provides a weather seal and, at the same time, forms a vertical drainage channel. Each high panel laps over each lower one and each joint is stiffened by a special T-bar which doubles up as a ladder rail.

This distribution centre has a significance beyond its architecture. The client was determined to continue the democratic ideals he had taken up at Bath for the workforce. All grades of staff mix freely in an undifferentiated series of spaces and the very flexibility of the building helps to make it responsive to the needs of the people who work in it.

Herman Miller Distribution Centre

Plan

1 pressed aluminium
  cladding
2 main entrance
3 future expansion
4 access to external seating
5 rest area
6 on-grade loading
7 dock loading
8 wc
9 dock office
10 vending
11 refuse
12 plant room
13 sprinkler pump room
14 sprinkler tank

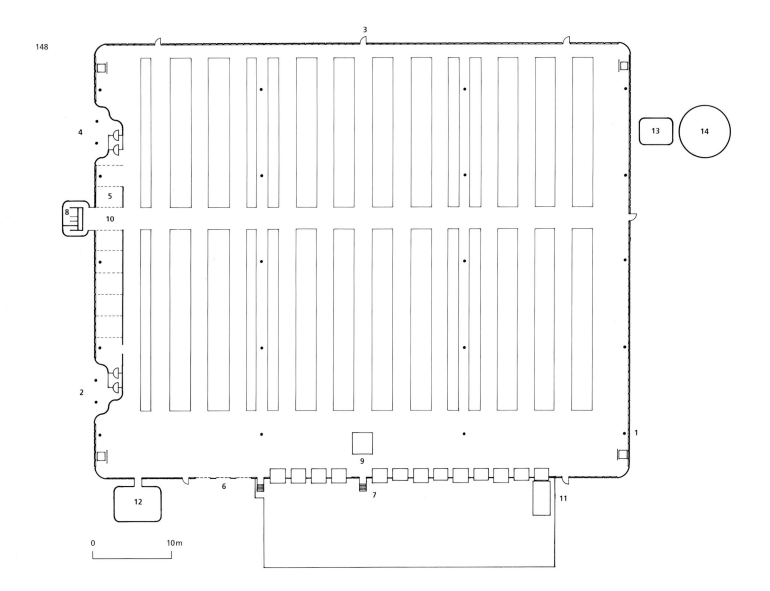

0   10m

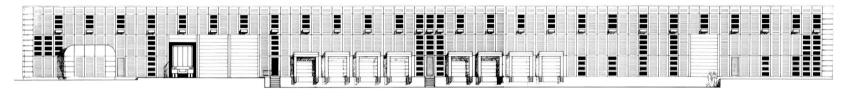

Herman Miller Distribution Centre

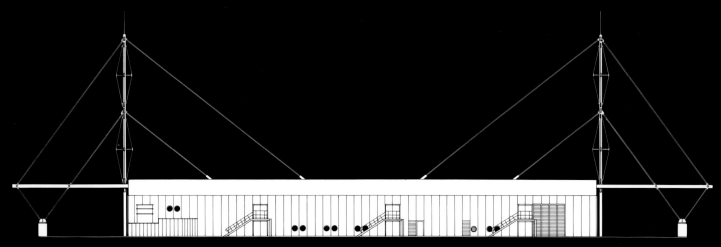

Ice Rink, Oxford, 1984

'Oxford City Council wanted a social centre
for the young people in the town. They
wanted an ice rink but only had two thirds of
the budget that was considered necessary.
They also wanted an exciting landmark
building that would attract people to it.

   'Our idea was a structural one. A spine beam
running the whole length of the building was
"hung" from two masts which themselves
made the building very noticeable. We saved
a lot of money by cladding the building with
cold store panels – this seemed appropriate
for an ice rink. Many finishes were omitted
with the hope that they would be
reinstated later.

   'The building today is a social centre for all
ages, and we have heard from the City
Engineer that vandalism has reduced
dramatically in the city since this project was
completed.' **NG**

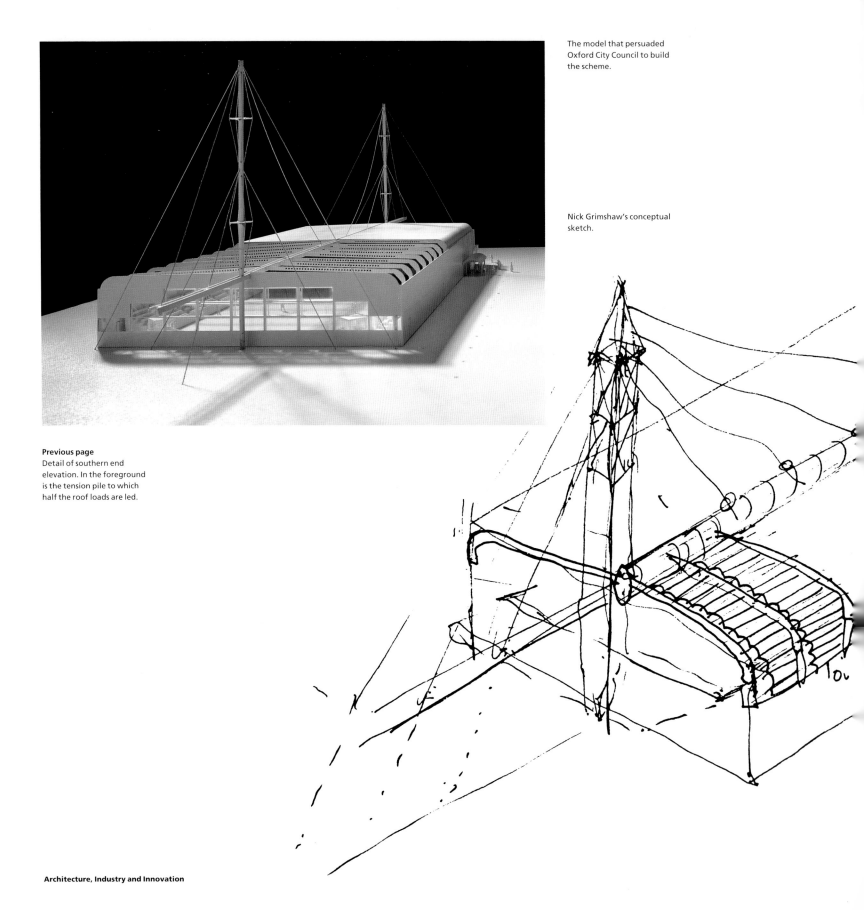

The model that persuaded
Oxford City Council to build
the scheme.

Nick Grimshaw's conceptual
sketch.

Previous page
Detail of southern end
elevation. In the foreground
is the tension pile to which
half the roof loads are led.

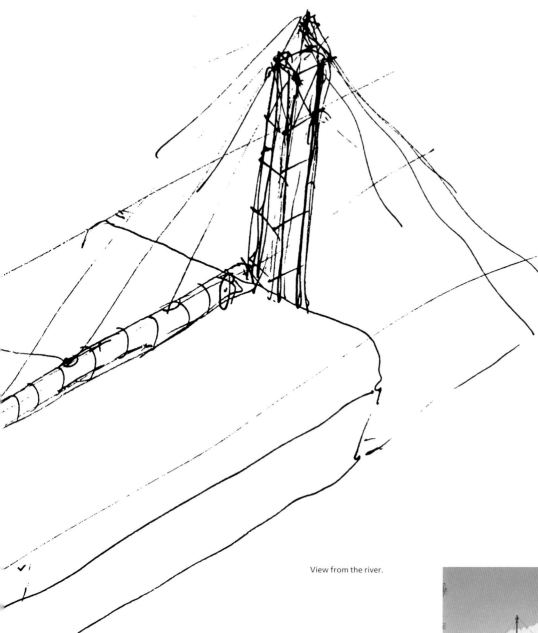

View from the river.

There is something marvellous about a public building where children and adults mix freely to enjoy their sport, and where there is virtually no vandalism despite intensive and almost constant use by large numbers of people.

The brief for this project came from a local authority, Oxford City Council, who wanted a sports facility on a site in the meadows to the west of the city. The new building had to act as its own advertisement and attract large numbers of users. The aim was for the facility to be self-financing as far as possible in terms of capital and running costs.

The site suffered from difficult ground conditions and piling was necessary. Because of this, the architects decided to take much of the weight of the necessarily wide-span roof up to a spine beam that is suspended

Ice Rink, Oxford

View from Oxpens Road.

from two tall masts. The frame provides a column-free space approximately 72m long by 38m wide allowing for a 56m x 26m ice pad. The two 30m-high masts are what Robert Venturi and Denise Scott Brown would call 'high readers'; they act as signs visible at a distance among the spires of Oxford.

The ice rink is enclosed by a panelled shell that has its own highpoint of drama in its entirely glazed north wall that renders the whole rink, with all its activity, visible to the outside world.

It is impossible not to draw nautical parallels when confronted by this building which has something of the character of a two-masted schooner. In fact, the building is already known locally as the 'Cutty Sark'. This nautical impression is reinforced by the approach to the rink – the visitor enters up a gently-sloping ramp which encourages the impression that you may be piped

South elevation.

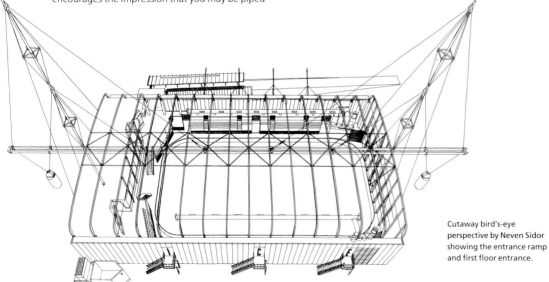

Cutaway bird's-eye perspective by Neven Sidor showing the entrance ramp and first floor entrance.

Architecture, Industry and Innovation

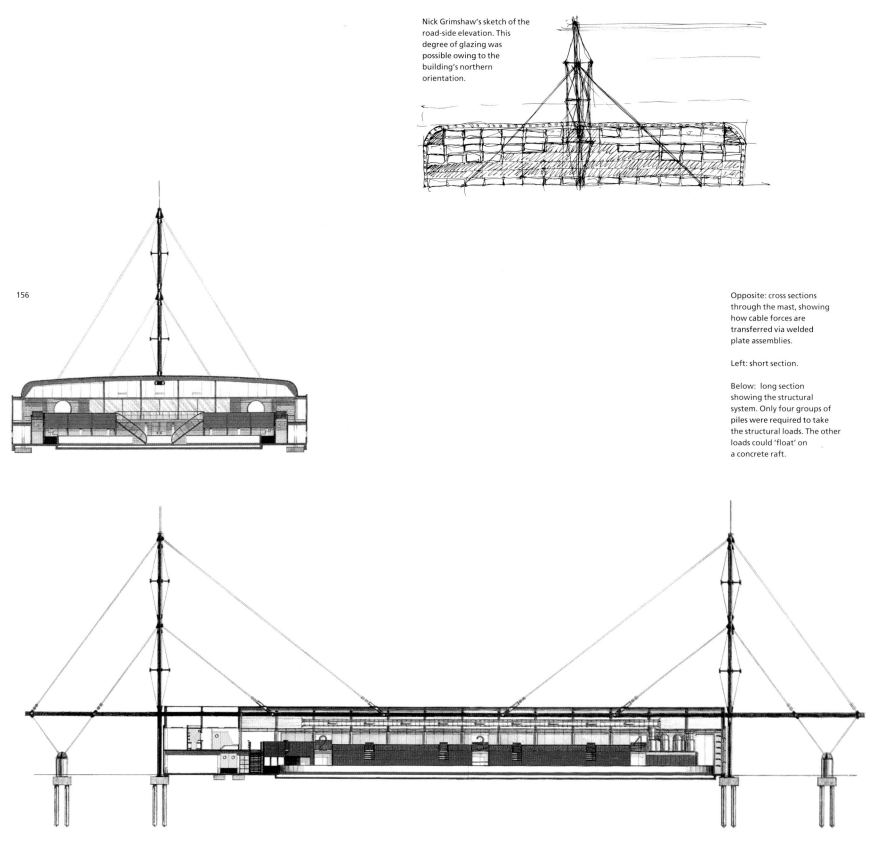

Nick Grimshaw's sketch of the road-side elevation. This degree of glazing was possible owing to the building's northern orientation.

Opposite: cross sections through the mast, showing how cable forces are transferred via welded plate assemblies.

Left: short section.

Below: long section showing the structural system. Only four groups of piles were required to take the structural loads. The other loads could 'float' on a concrete raft.

156

Architecture, Industry and Innovation

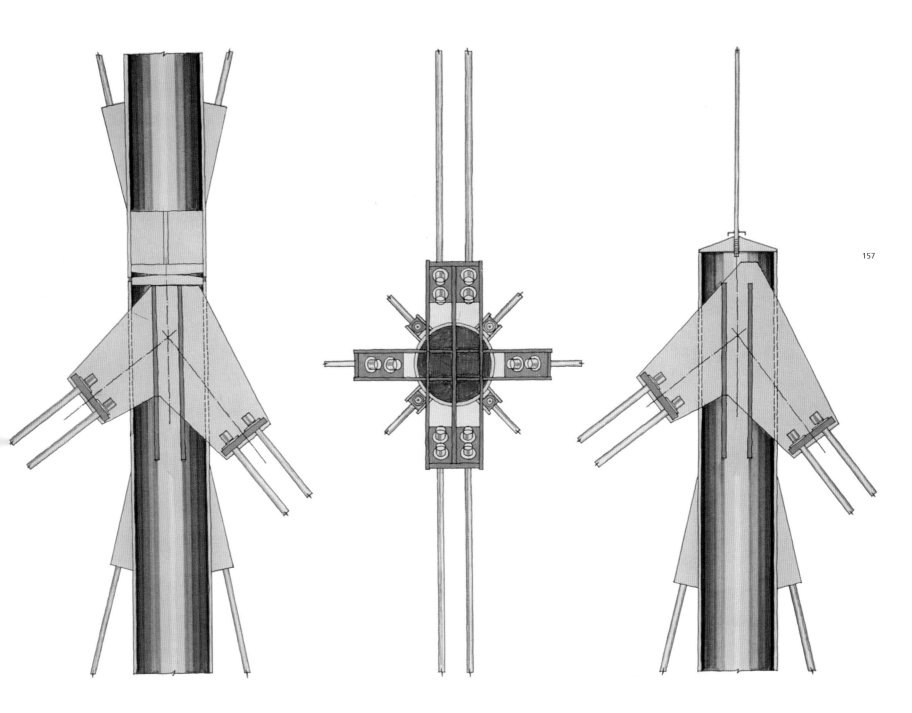

Ice Rink, Oxford

The principle of a first floor entrance separates 'dry' spectator activities from 'wet' skater activities.

aboard. Of course, all the external structure is justified by the functional needs of a weighty building on a somewhat marshy site. Saarinen at Yale saw the opportunity for an expressive building in his ice hockey rink – the need for a huge uncluttered space for the rink led him to design an inspired roof structure.

From the users' point of view, all that matters is that there is a large enough sweep of uninterrupted ice. Grimshaw succeeds brilliantly on this front. Inside the building it is the ice that dominates. His plan means that everything is near the ice – the boot changing, the spectators, the bleachers – everything is close at hand. There is the added benefit of a great deal of aural as well as visual excitement. The perpetual sound of steel blades on ice reverberates excitingly throughout the building, permeating the upper level bar, shop and function rooms.

The structural solution adopted employs a spine beam to pick up the majority of the roof load, which is transmitted to the masts at either end of the building; under each mast there is a group of only four piles. Loads from the spine beam are transmitted to the masts via stainless steel rods and the masts are stabilized by anchoring them to the building's edge beam with 'bowsprit' struts, thus avoiding the need to pile the entire site. The spine beam is formed from a pair of rectangular box-sections, and is hung by tension rods which result in a single large compression load and tension load at each end of the building. Rib beams span across the building at 4.8m centres.

This Oxford building is a visual and structural *tour de force* – and its commercial success is almost certainly linked to the exciting drawing power of the architecture.

Ice Rink, Oxford

Section through entrance
1 fixed tip-up seats
2 retractable bleacher
  seating
3 fixed tractor seats
4 rink barrier
5 ice pad
6 entrance kiosk
7 entrance bridge frame
8 entrance canopy

160

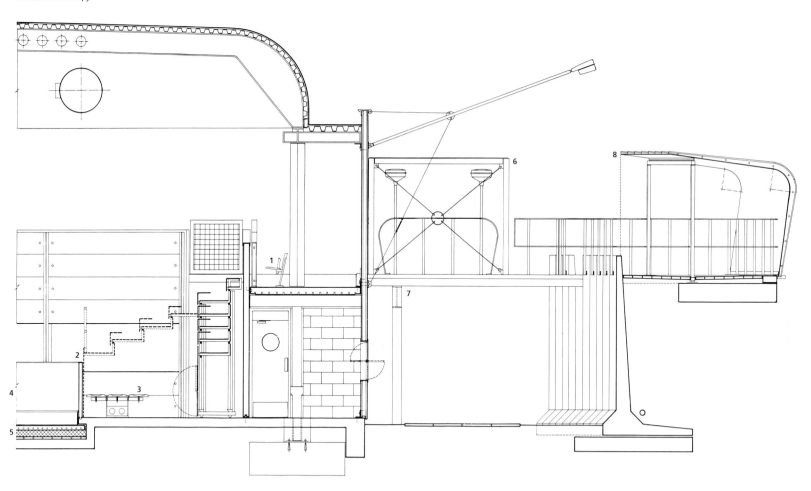

Ground floor plan

1 ice pit/ice machine garage
2 air plant
3 professional changing rooms
4 first aid
5 cafeteria
6 catering manager
7 food store
8 kitchen
9 servery
10 bottle store
11 cleaner stores
12 female wc
13 male wc
14 skate store
15 ice plant
16 water storage
17 lv switchroom
18 skate hire
19 tuck shop
20 staff changing rooms
21 boiler room
22 instructors
23 disco control/judges, etc
24 fixed seating
25 rink store

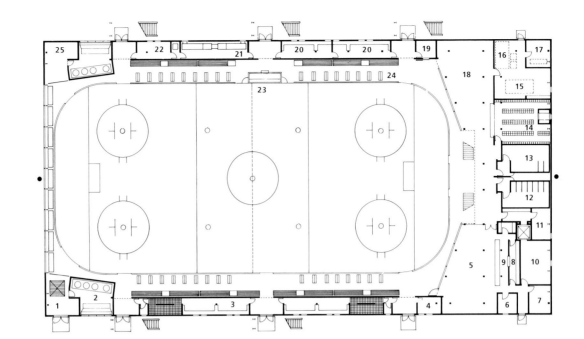

First floor plan

1 1 in 25 entrance ramp
2 entrance canopy
3 ticket kiosk
4 bridge
5 lessons desk
6 administrative office
7 manager's office
8 shop
9 bar
10 raised bar viewing area
11 bar stores
12 cleaner stores
13 disabled wc
14 male wc
15 female wc
16 conference room
17 bleacher seating
18 transformer enclosure
19 cooling tower
20 fixed seating
21 gallery

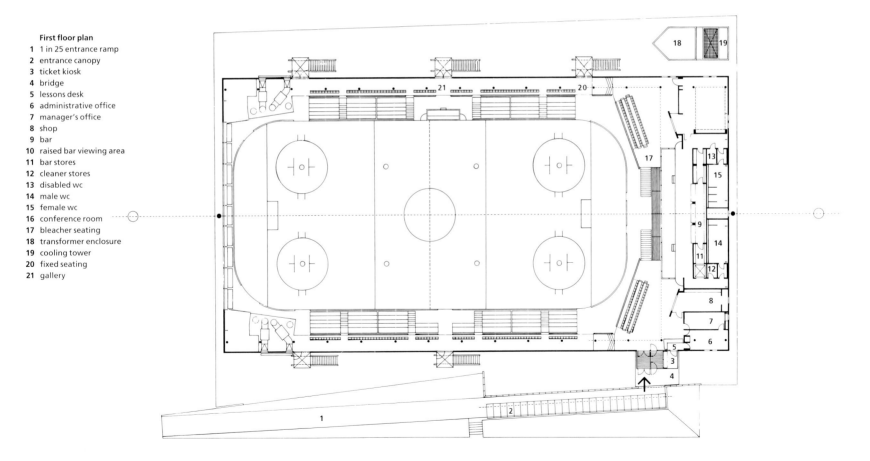

0   10m

Ice Rink, Oxford

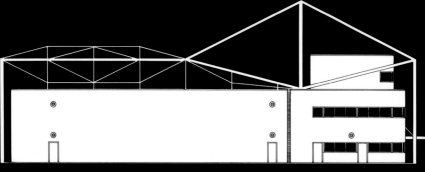

**Headquarters for Ladkarn,
London Docklands, 1985**

'This earth-moving company, based under
the railway arches in South London, wanted
to expand and build themselves a new
headquarters. They took the London
Docklands Development Corporation at its
word when it said it wanted to encourage
new business in this enterprise zone. They
applied for one of the best sites at the edge
of the water facing a vast empty quay.

'The brief was relatively simple, offices
and ancillary facilities and a vast clear-span
workshop for servicing lorries and earth-
moving equipment. An external structure
seemed obvious in this case as no internal
obstructions could be accepted. We
decided to express the 30m clear spans.
These were formed from tubes which were
only 150mm in diameter and we allowed them
to fly freely above the roof, rather like the
bow-sprits of old sailing ships. The client
was delighted and felt that the company had
a real headquarters at last.' **NG**

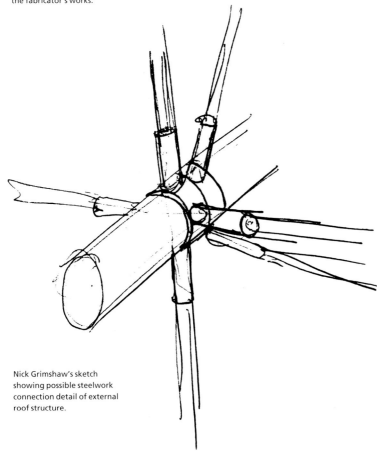

Nick Grimshaw's sketch
showing possible steelwork
connection detail of external
roof structure.

Nick Grimshaw's early
compositional sketch.

The idea of providing a headquarters building for a firm
of hauliers, earth-movers and muck-shifters, that would
have as much elegance as a Grimshaw building for IBM
or BMW, was an interesting challenge. There were other
unusual things about the brief: the site was in London's
Docklands – an Enterprise Zone, technically free of
planning restrictions, but not free of bureaucracy – and
the client wanted a fixed price for his new building.

The original site was at the north-east corner of the
West India Dock – an important position surrounded by
water on three sides. Later, because of the rampant
expansion of Canary Wharf, the building had to be
moved and re-erected on another site within three years
of its completion. The decision to move to the Beckton
site, some three miles to the east of the original site, was
made easier by the possibility of re-using the structure
and many of the other elements of the building.

In architectural terms, the brief was one with which
the architects were familiar. The client wanted a huge
column-free area as a vehicle maintenance workshop
with ancillary offices and services areas backing it up. In
addition to performing well as workshops and offices,
the client expected his premises to be an advertisement
for his company. The decision to design a masted
structural system that would be both dramatic and
highly visible while providing the necessary clear span
for the workshops, provided a swift and universal
solution to these challenges.

Conceptually, the office and workshop facility
consists of three almost separate steel-framed
structures. The 653m² office building is framed
conventionally with concrete floors which act as plates
to distribute horizontal loads. It is not dependent for its

View across dock towards
front elevation showing the
three floors of offices.

Previous page
View across roof showing
external structure. By cross
bracing in four directions a
tube of only 150mm diameter
was able to span 30 metres.

Roof plan illustrating external
structure and roof terrace.

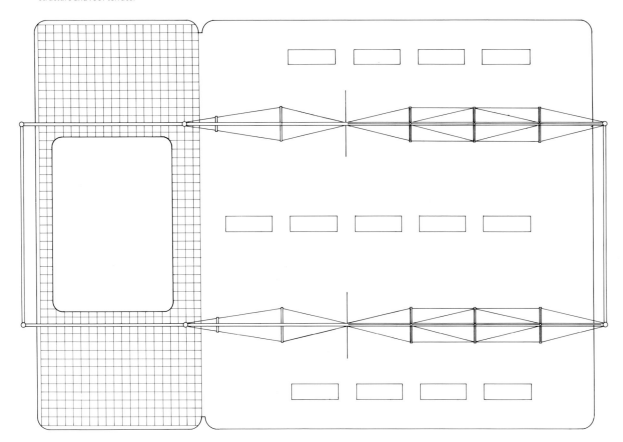

0   10m

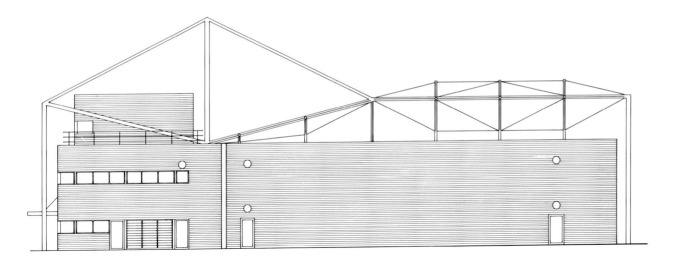

East elevation

South elevation

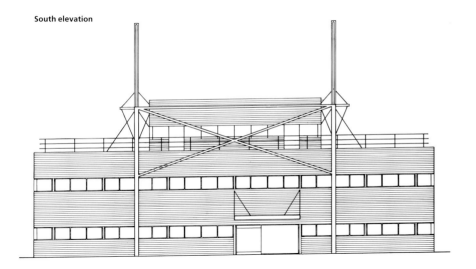

stability on either of the other two structures.

The 899m² workshop block relies on the external steel frame for vertical support at 12 internal suspension points, lateral stability being provided partly by diagonal braced bays and partly by the office building. The beams support the roof decking directly without the use of purlins and are continuous and pin-jointed to the columns.

The external steel structure consists of a continuous 'boom' – which is stabilized by tension rods and cross members. The deflection in this boom is reduced by the provision of tension members which pass over the roof of the ancillary office building and down to the ground in front of it.

The masts are propped at second floor level by a connection to the office building. Fore and mizzen masts cantilever from the bases and are connected by a hollow section truss at high level. These structural elements are painted red while the cladding system for the warehouses and offices is of profiled silver steel sheeting.

The imagery of the river, docks, shipping and masts is part of the story of this company headquarters and the architecture is functional and, at the same time, appropriately contextual.

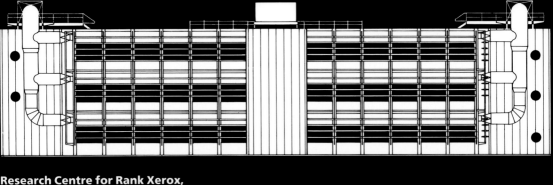

**Research Centre for Rank Xerox,
Welwyn Garden City, 1988**

'Xerox urgently required a research facility
and commissioned us to carry out a feasibility
study to look at several sites on their industrial
campus in Welwyn.

'As a multi-disciplinary team of architects
and engineers, we visited the West Coast of
America for briefing sessions. We discovered

View across Bessemer Road looking towards west elevation.

Below: site location plan.

Bottom: exterior view of north-east elevation.

173

A client with enormous experience of manufacturing and selling sophisticated technology provided the practice with its first major commission for an office building. Rank Xerox Research needed 4,300m^2 of highly-serviced space to house 200 systems engineers and their support staff on a site at Welwyn Garden City adjacent to the company's other manufacturing activities.

In many ways, the problems and opportunities offered by this commission were typical of the challenges that any expanding company in the high technology research fields faces when confronted with need for new accommodation. Much of the company's future work is, by nature, relatively unknown and the client expected that some 20% to 25% of their floor space may have to be replanned and re-equipped every year. This high degree of flexibility meant that the architects and engineers were really designing a highly-serviced shelter and space for an infinite variety of uses. In October 1987, at the time of the building's completion, Nick Grimshaw wrote in the Rank Xerox house journal *Insight*: 'Total flexibility is the name of the game. In discussion with our clients we agreed that because it is difficult to predict the future direction of such a fast-developing business, the building should be designed so that anything can happen anywhere!'

The solution for this facility was based upon a 12m-deep, column-free accommodation with a central atrium that rises the full height of the three-storey building. Six service towers around the perimeter of the block house the lavatories, escape stairs, coffee areas and conference rooms. The crucial factor for the researchers working here was the provision of 100%

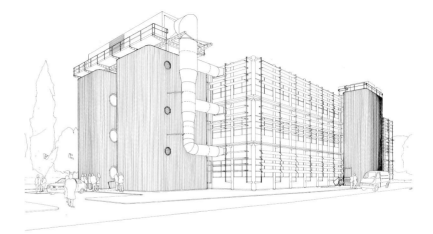

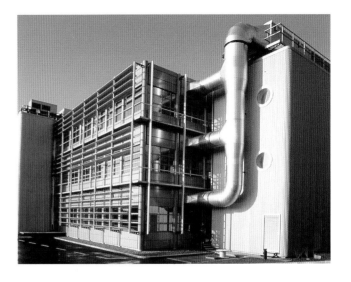

Research Centre for Rank Xerox

View along exterior catwalk.

Detailed view of north-east corner of the building.

accessible cabling in the raised floor throughout the building, and generous service risers. A 1.5m grid running throughout the building governs the disposition of structure, services and finishes alike.

There were also important environmental considerations that acted as determinants of the design – the need for suitable and safe environments for computers and good lighting conditions for those working on VDU screens. The building's deep plan made an atrium necessary for the provision of daylight, as well as for the centralizing of circulation between floors. In architectural terms, the client wanted a new building that would in itself attract recruits and encourage the development of a sense of community among all the research workers.

In construction terms, the building is very simple. It is a steel-framed building with lightweight concrete floors on profiled metal decking. For ease and accuracy of construction, the majority of individual elements were fabricated off site. The two problems that needed

Part elevation.

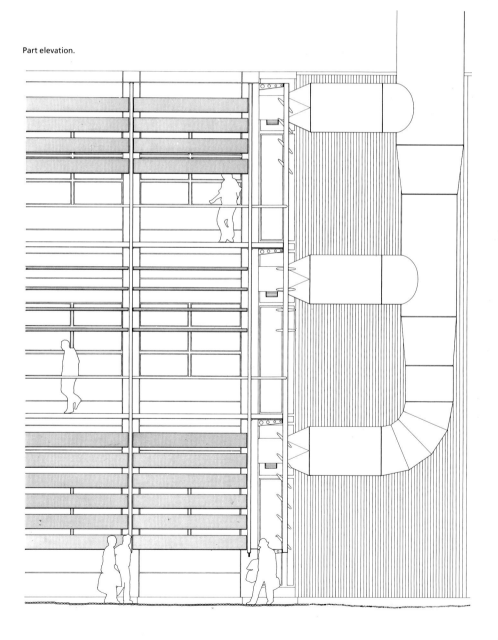

Architecture, Industry and Innovation

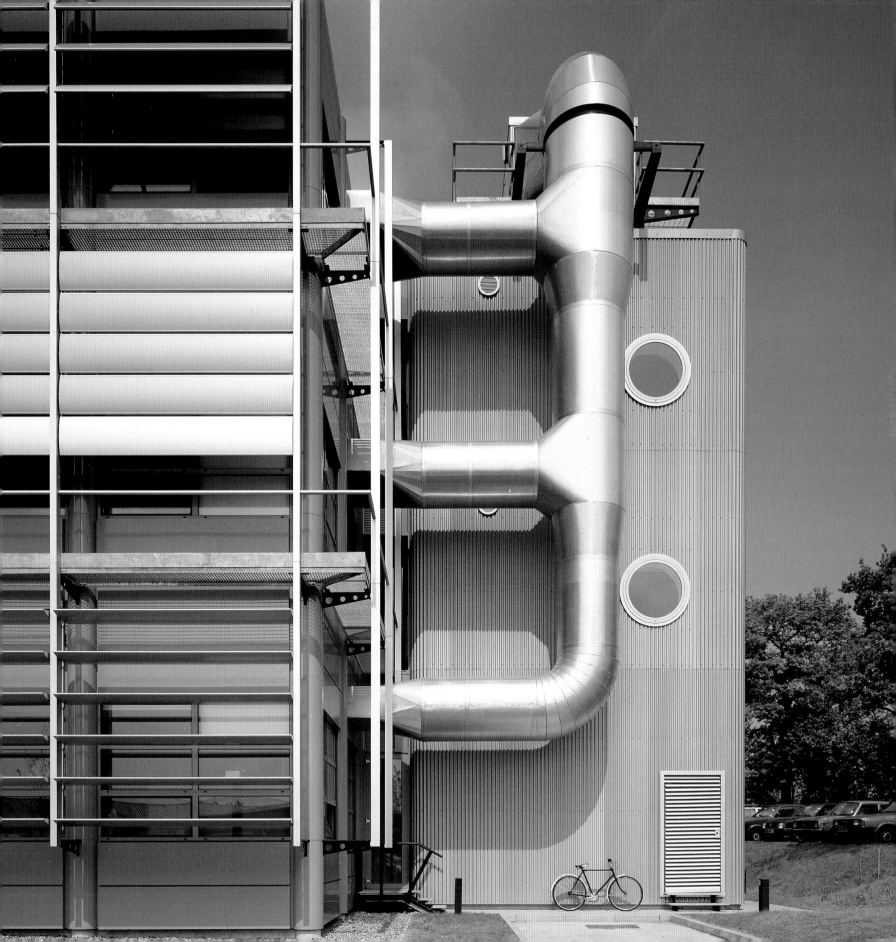

View up atrium stairs.

Detailed section.

View of south-east corner.

special solutions – light in the offices and air conditioning for the whole environment – were solved, in the first instance, by external motorized louvres to provide a glare-free working office, and in the second by the provision of air handling and chilling units on the roof. External ducts to serve all floors make a dramatic appearance on the outside of the building. The provision of effective light and air in working buildings is an age-old architectural problem. Here the two solutions help each other – by shading the outside of the building solar gain is halved. This does not solve the entire problem of heat gain associated with masses of high-tech machinery; however, the consequent loading on the air cooling can be reduced. The result is an effective machine for working in.

177

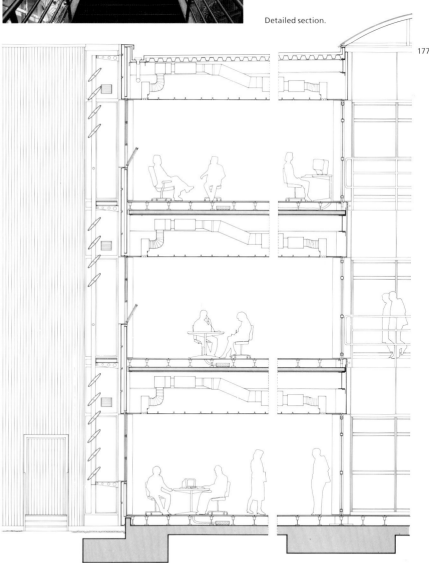

Research Centre for Rank Xerox

Plan
1 open-plan
 accommodation
2 pod arranged as
 conference room and wcs
3 pod arranged as wcs only

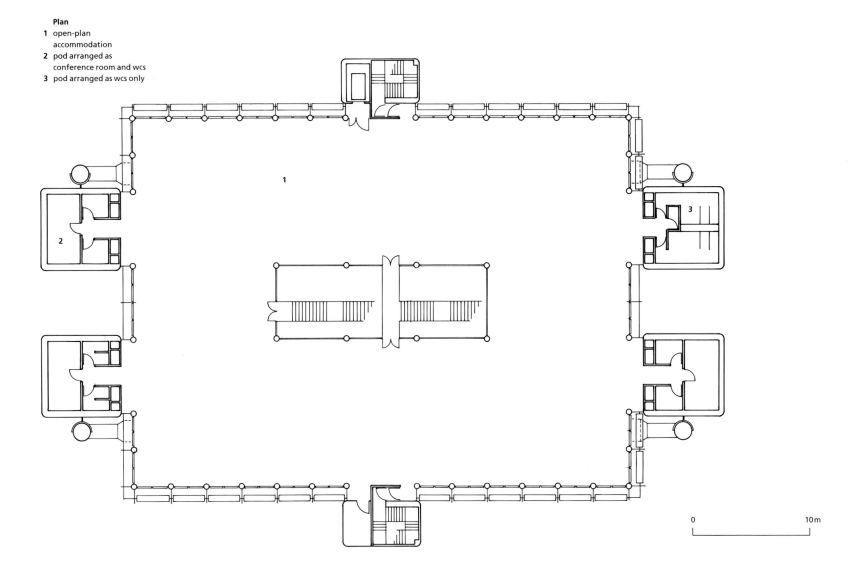

0   10m

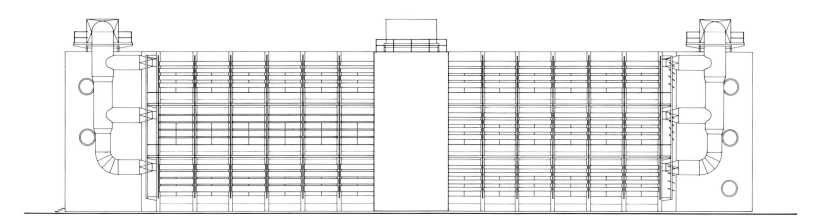

East elevation

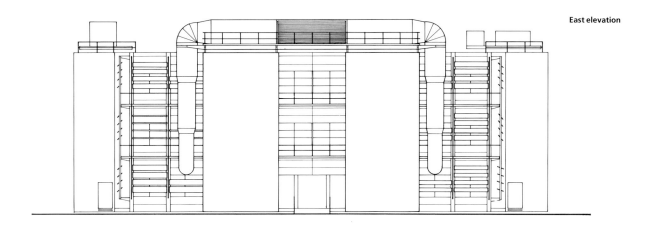

Research Centre for Rank Xerox

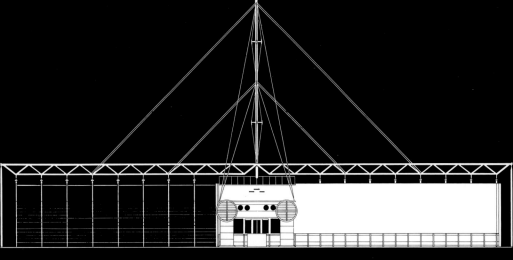

Leisure Centre, Stockbridge, 1986–88

'The site was at the centre of a regeneration
area focused on one of the worst areas of
decentralized housing outside Liverpool. The
government had finally realized that it was
not enough simply to provide housing for
people and that a solid back-up of shopping,
leisure facilities and, of course, work
opportunities were needed as well.

Elevation showing leisure
pool on the right and the
open sports area on the left.
This was to form an enclosed
sports hall at a later phase.

Original sketch by Nick
Grimshaw exploring the idea
of a masted structure which
would signal the building
from a long distance away.

182

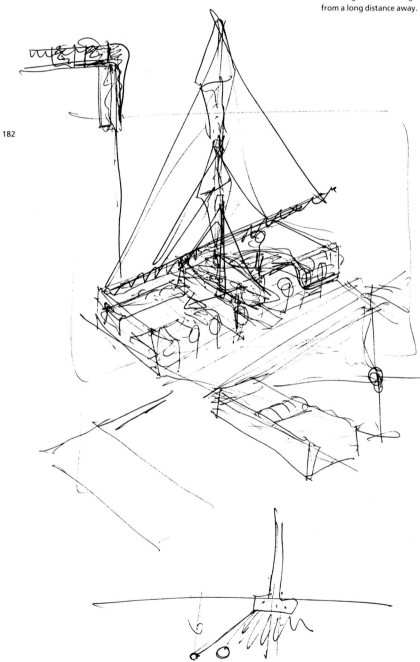

Detailed view of the front
entrance.

Early sketch by Nick Grimshaw
showing a possible
combination between ribbed
metal cladding and a panel
system for the lower part of
the building.

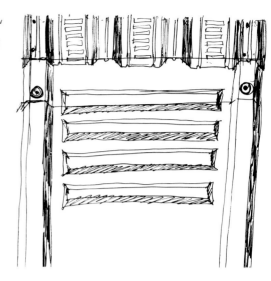

Detailed view of the open
play area which was planned
to be enclosed at a later date.

185

There is a clear relationship between this community
sports building and the ice rink at Oxford. In each case,
the client was a local council and both wanted
reasonably inexpensive but efficient buildings with a
high architectural profile. But the pool and sports
building in Stockbridge Village at Knowsley near
Liverpool was commissioned in special circumstances
– after the 1982 Toxteth riots – as part of a campaign
to transform some of that city's most deprived areas.
Vandalized tower blocks were replaced by low-rise
housing, and this leisure centre was intended as a
symbol of more constructive times.

Chronologically, the leisure centre belongs with
Oxford's rink and structurally it is closely related. Large
spans were needed to create the column-free spaces for
the pool and the 'dry' activities in the future sports hall,
and so an external structure was used for the primary
members. A central mast supports an external delta
truss, suspended over the ridge, from which arched ribs
span out to form the enclosure and support the building
envelope. Thus the ribs act not as a portal frame, which
would require much deeper rib members, but as a pin
structure. The mast forms a landmark in the
neighbourhood and provides a dramatic part of the
building's design; it plunges through the centre of the
building and is flanked by stairs and a lift.

The plan for the completed building (the sports hall
remains to be built inside its waiting structure) makes
the social and administrative rooms the centre of the
building, serving both 'wet' and 'dry' activities. The

Leisure Centre, Stockbridge

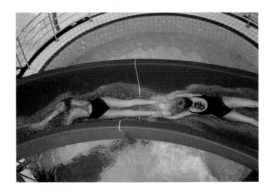

Two swimmers trying out the water slide before the opening of the building. (NB once the building was in operation a strict rule of 'only one person on the slide at a time' was applied.)

A surprisingly lifelike early model showing the wave pool and the water slide in action.

basement contains water filtration and air handling plant, the ground floor houses the changing rooms that are on the same level as the various pools, and there are bars and vending areas on the entrance floor which provide casual viewing areas for parents and spectators to watch the activities in the pools below. A top floor is used exclusively for staff and management providing secure monitoring for the whole building.

One of the requirements of the brief was that the building should be as vandal-proof as possible – without looking as though it was fortified. This has been achieved; the concrete plinth protects the building and the tough, but not unsympathetic, cladding has clearly been designed to survive. A peculiarly local requirement was that the structure should be able to resist a car being driven into the building and then set on fire. The garden at the pool end of the building is enclosed with a fence constructed of motorway crash barriers for a similar reason. Inside, the building provides the now familiar 'leisure pool' facilities, with wave machines, beaches and flumes. The client's wish to create a tropical paradise inside this efficient, well-serviced and cleanly detailed building was achieved without too much incongruity.

The pool in its early days of usage. Note the waves beginning to form and the gently sloping floor.

Ground floor plan
1 reception
2 vending
3 bar
4 main pool
5 children's pool
6 splash pool
7 water slide
8 pool garden

188

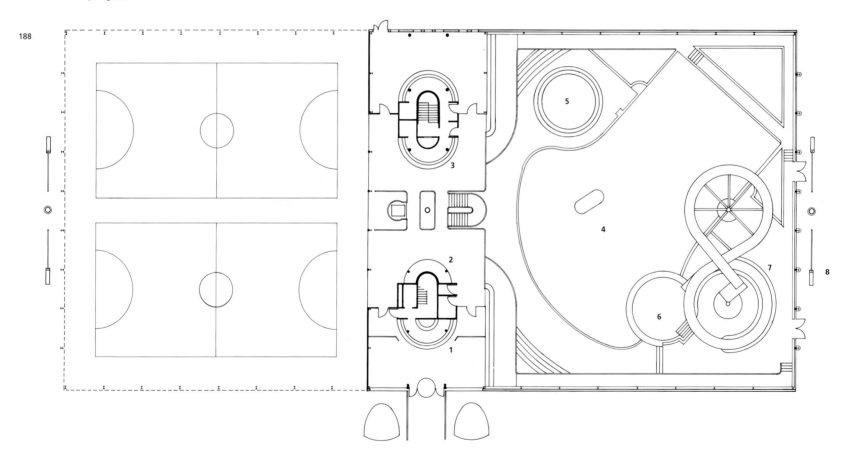

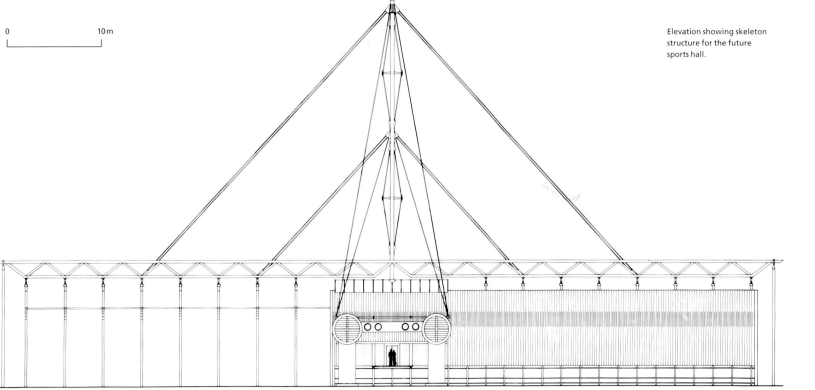

Elevation showing skeleton
structure for the future
sports hall.

0   10m

Leisure Centre, Stockbridge

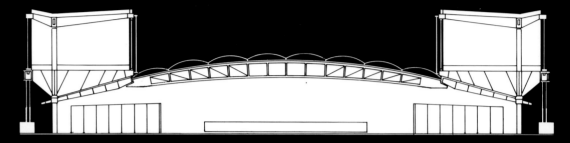

**Superstore for Sainsbury's, Camden,
London, 1986–88**

'Sainsbury's were having trouble getting
planning permission for a superstore in
Camden Town and asked us to take on the job.
We contacted the planners for an explanation.
"All we want is a good piece of modern
architecture" they said. "Sainsbury's architects
have tried LEB Georgian, By-Pass-Tudor,
Surrey Farmhouse and even some kind of
high-tech pastiche, but none of these schemes
were any good."

   'We took on board Sainsbury's rigorous
operational requirements, including the
exact dimensions required for the store,
the loading and food preparation. Most
importantly we dealt with their demanding
requirements for car parking. Then we built
a model of the building in its context. Camden
Planning Committee passed the scheme and
Sainsbury's were delighted.

   'As a whole, this was our first urban design
project. It incorporated a crèche, workshops
and a row of canalside houses. Thus a whole
city block was redeveloped.

   'Successful – the store most certainly is.
Whether this is due to the car park, the food
or the architecture I imagine will always
depend on whether you are a driver,
a gourmet or an architect.' **NG**

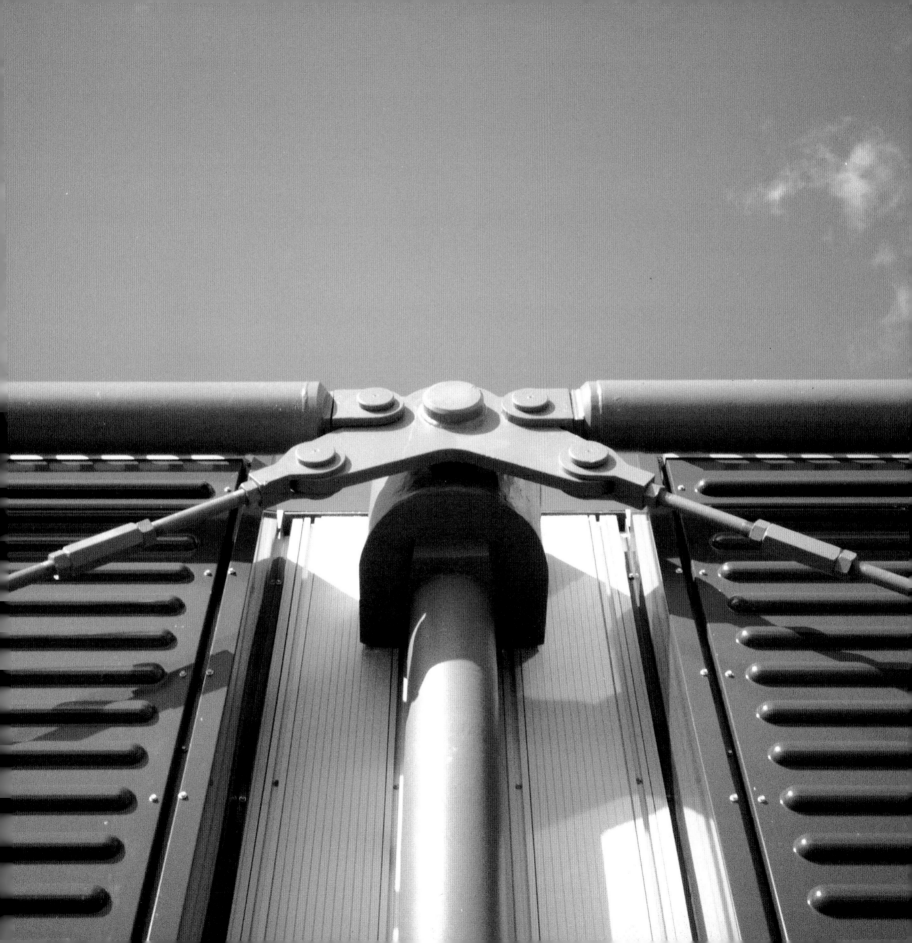

The exposed 'emergency truss' meets the tip of one of the cantilevered brackets.

Left: the exposed structural system enriches the street.

Right: Nick Grimshaw's sketch showing structural concept.

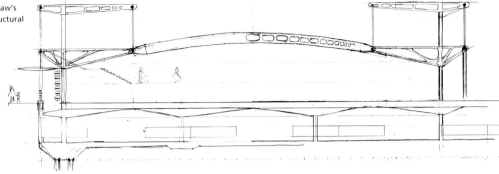

Site model showing the store in relation to a row of Georgian houses and a small Gothic revival church. The loading area is encircled by workshops and houses. The structural grid of the new store evoked the party wall rhythm of the houses opposite. The top of the cladding also lined up with the cornice line of the houses.

How far is it possible to re-design the everyday things in life? When the Grimshaw office received the commission to design a supermarket for a difficult inner city site that had been occupied by a bakery and was bordered by three major London roads and a canal, they entered a difficult arena. The planners wanted a sophisticated modern building, as well as comprehensive redevelopment to reverse the blight on the entire site. There was a planning agreement for some housing and workshops, as well as the need for parking to be on two levels. The requirements for supermarkets are strict and in much of the UK it is a conservative building type.

The practice brought to the task the experience they had gained in the design of a multitude of column-free spaces, and considerable experience of the demands of commercial clients for infinitely flexible spaces. This was Grimshaw's first retail commission and he brought to it a freshness of view. He felt that a good precedent was the 'market hall' approach and looked back at some of the great 19th-century cast iron examples. Grimshaw's supermarket has an elegantly curved roof

193

Cantilevered plate girders along Camden Road make what would have been a two storey building appear more than three storeys high. In this way an out-of-town building type matched its new urban context without deceit.

over the main shopping hall which represented a complete breakthrough for the client. To achieve the 43.2m roof span, the roof is supported by cantilevers that are steadied by 'columns' of clustered tie rods. On the Camden Road elevation, these columned bays echo the scale of the shops and houses on the opposite side of the street, which have the standard London late-Georgian width between party walls of 20 feet. The height of the store, with staff accommodation and storage at the first floor, generally ties in with the cornice line of the terraces of Georgian buildings and the expressive structure is not out of place next door to the flying buttresses of the neighbouring Gothic revival church.

Cutaway isometric by Simon Templeton.

Partially covered court where shoppers are assembled, whether they have parked below or above ground, before entering the store. The canopy structure responds to the flying buttresses of the adjoining church.

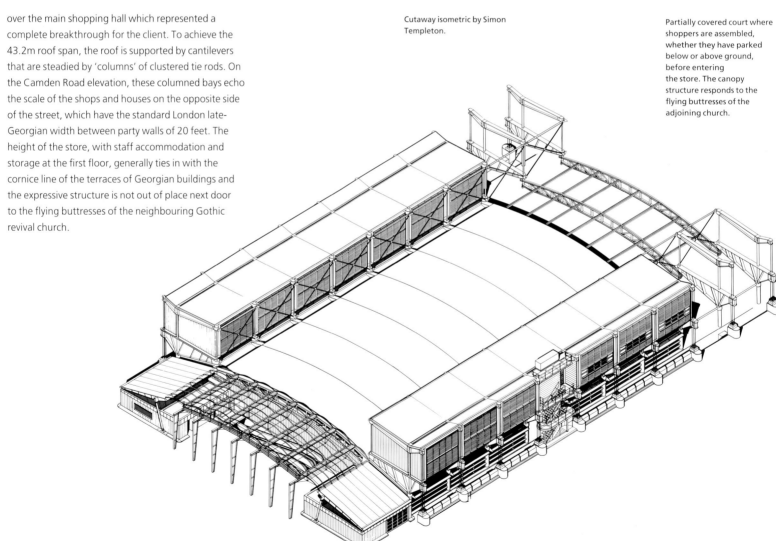

Fire exit staircase, Camden
Road. Note how the ground
and first floor are separated
by a strip of daylight coming
from the store roof behind.

All exposed steelwork is given
two hour's fire resistance
using an intumescent epoxy
coating. This was crucial to
maintaining the building's
plate girder aesthetic.

While the store is a celebration of structure, it has
innovative features that have allowed it to be so
expressive; for example the use of new forms of fire
protection. A 12mm-thick coating of a special
epoxy/ceramic material (developed for nuclear waste
containers) allows the main cantilever beam to
withstand fire for up to two hours. Similarities of scale
help the building to settle into its urban surroundings,
but in every other aspect the building stands alone. The
materials are metal and glass, and the upper floors have
grey pressed-aluminium panels with horizontal strip-
windows. The ground floor shop front on the Camden
Road is one long glazed wall which allows an
uninterrupted view from the street of the entire shop,
and also allows staff working at the check-out desks to
have some contact with the outside world. This is in
marked contrast to the endless blank walls of so many
supermarkets. Another relatively rare event in a
superstore is the provision of a travolator to link the
store to the underground car park. A simple adaptation
of the wheels of the shopping trolleys makes it possible

Sainsbury Superstore, Camden

Hin Tan, one of the project
architects, in front of one of
the plate girders with the
foreman at the steelworks.

The cladding system
developed for the Herman
Miller building at
Chippenham was developed
further and used for this
project.

Structural forces are
transferred at the outer tip of
every plate girder.

to anchor them to the moving travolator so that it is easy
to move large loads from one level to another.

As part of the whole urban planning exercise, the
architects and the clients were asked to provide housing
along the canal (see page 204), workshops and a
crèche. The light industrial workshops were placed on
the Kentish Town Road some two storeys up (to allow
the passage of large delivery vehicles beneath) in a
simple concrete-framed building. From this
development, the local community has gained not just
6,000m^2 of supermarket, but also a complete mixture of
uses on the site – shopping, housing, light industry, a
crèche, some small retail units and a coffee shop, as well
as parking for 300 cars.

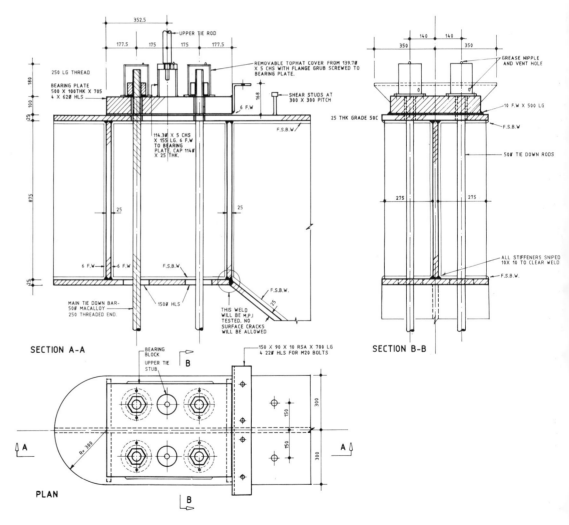

The complete structural system is visible along the Camden Street elevation. Many hours were spent detailing the cladding so that no structural element would be lost.

200   The 'emergency truss' facing the central roof means that any one plate girder could fail without catastrophe.

Working drawings showing the plate girder inner tip where the central roof trusses are supported.

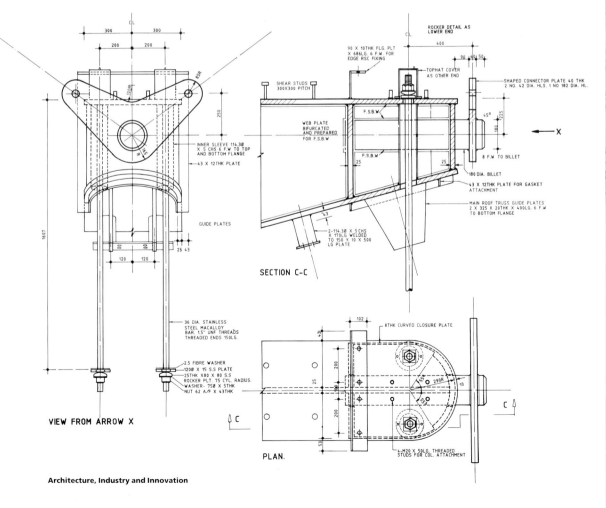

VIEW FROM ARROW X

SECTION C-C

PLAN.

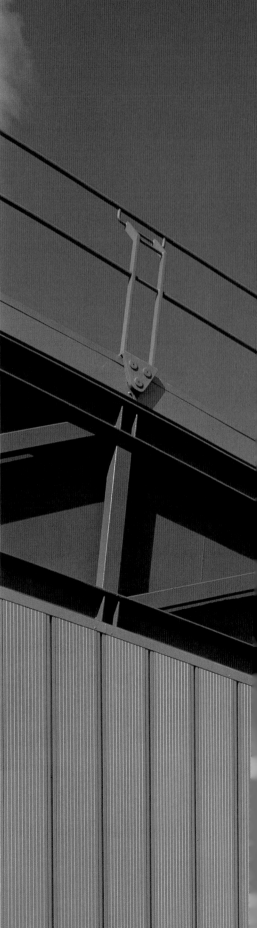

Architecture, Industry and Innovation

Site plan
1 car park
2 ramp to basement
3 service yard
4 back up
5 bakery
6 tea room
7 sales area
8 entrance mall
9 workshop yard
10 shop

0   20m

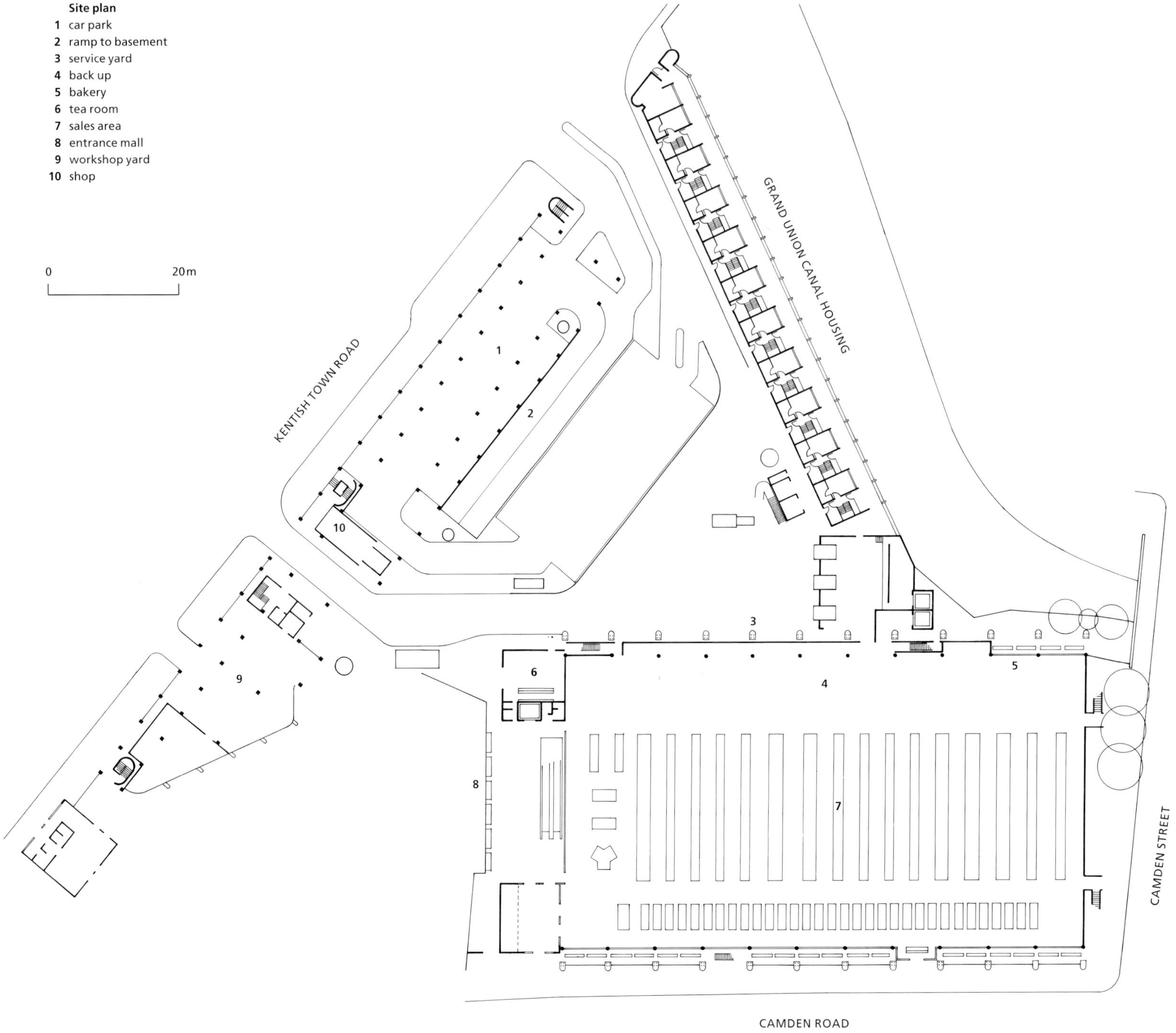

KENTISH TOWN ROAD

GRAND UNION CANAL HOUSING

CAMDEN STREET

CAMDEN ROAD

1

2

10

3

4

5

6

8

7

9

Sections through supermarket and entrance atrium

1 supermarket sales area
2 car park
3 travolator access to car park (also for use of specially-designed supermarket trolleys)
4 staff amenities
5 storage
6 coffee bar
7 entrance area

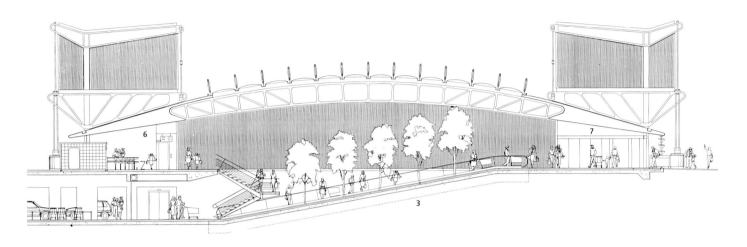

0   5m

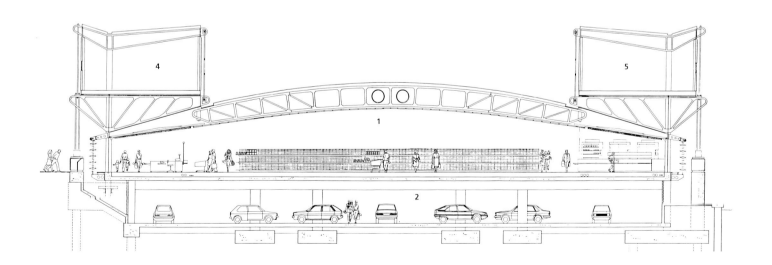

Sainsbury Superstore, Camden

**Houses at Grand Union Walk,
Camden, London, 1986–88**

'These houses were our first opportunity to do
a complete interior. They were a spin-off from
the superstore development and Sainsbury's
were happy that we had converted the
permission, originally for a block of flats, into a
row of freehold houses which by definition
were of much greater value.

　'We felt that the houses might well be
occupied by professionals, so a "professional"
room was designed with direct access from the
canalside walk. With its own bathroom
attached, this room could equally well be a
spare bedroom. The stairway led to a
magnificent north-facing double-height
studio living room, which would have
delighted an artist from the old Camden
Town school.

　'England has overwhelmingly pursued a
traditional approach to the house, particularly
since the War, whereas in the US, Europe and
Australia many fine examples of 20th-century
houses exist. With this modest addition of
canalside houses we felt that we had at least
made a positive gesture towards what is
possible in modern housing today.' **NG**

The access walkway leading
to all front doors is reached
via a street gate controlled by
an entryphone system.

Isometric showing three
houses. All windows plus
balconies face the canal. The
back wall was designed to
exclude all noise from the
supermarket loading bay.

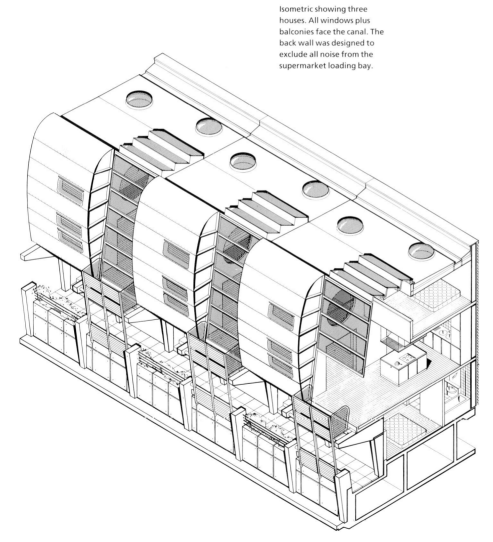

As part of the Sainsbury's supermarket development,
and under the terms of the planning agreement with
Camden Council, the client agreed to build some
private housing on a 10m-wide site alongside the
Grand Union Canal.

The development comprises a terrace of 10 three-
bedroom houses, a one-bedroom maisonette and a
bedsitting-room flat, all of which sit directly alongside
the canal. The absence of any south-facing windows,
due to the blind wall which faces the supermarket
yard, meant that the architects had to provide light
from a north-facing double-height glazed wall and
organize the plan so that the living space on the first
floor could be top-lit.

Housing is an unusual area for Grimshaw's practice
and they have applied much of their technical expertise
in a way that is, for English speculative housing, highly
innovative. The houses employ the technology of the
light industrial unit, and are adventurous and free of
domestic clichés. On the canal side, each house has
an insulated, curved metal wall punctured by windows
reminiscent of a fragment of an aeroplane. In between
each of these 'wings' there is a great full-height
aluminium-framed glass wall which is electrically
controlled and opens to allow the double-height dining
space to be used as part of a large open space that, in
the summer, includes the canal side balcony. Electrically-
operated aluminium blinds give privacy and protect the
glass wall from solar gain and glare.

The construction of the houses is a simple system of
concrete blockwork party walls with pre-cast concrete
floors and roofs pitched at 10°. Internally, the walls are
plastered and painted white, and natural beech is used
for stairs, flooring and other details.

The double-height living area becomes a garden on warm days, with the electric glazed doors in their raised position.

Main living area. Timber softens the technology.

Cross section: the ground floor is raised above the access towpath for privacy.

Open-plan living area with kitchen beyond.

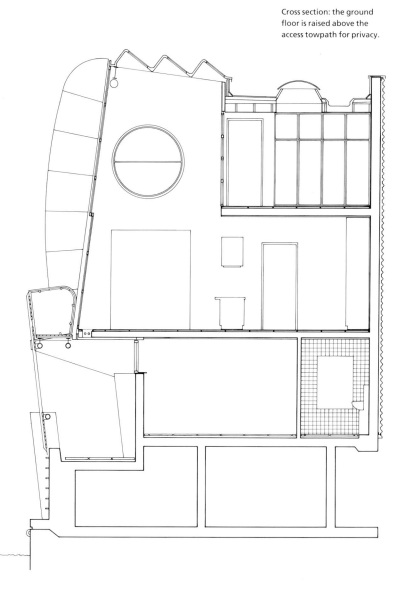

Architecture, Industry and Innovation

Canalside elevation
1 access route
2 glazed dining and balcony
3 curved aluminium cladding on living room and master bedroom

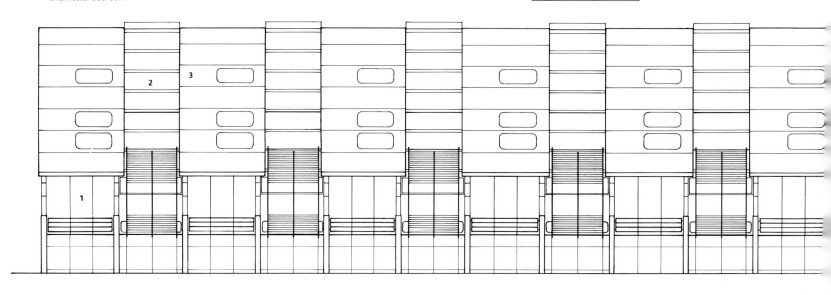

Second floor plan
1 bathroom
2–4 bedrooms

First floor plan
5 laundry
6 kitchen
7 dining room
8 living room

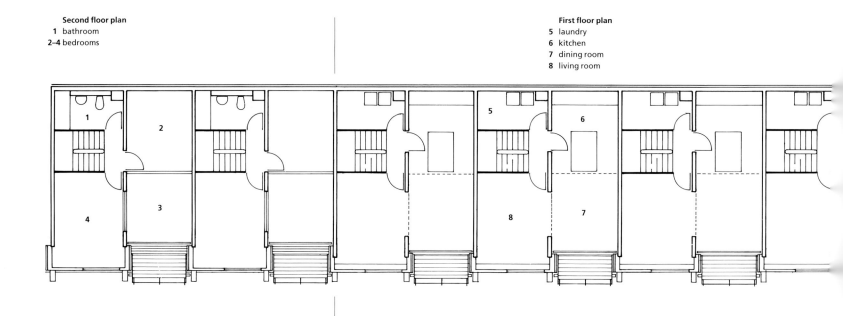

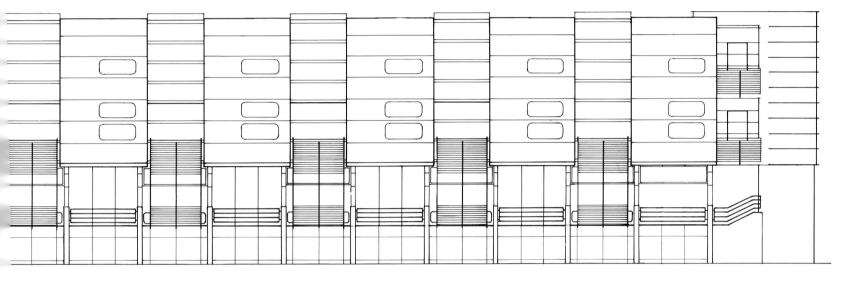

Ground floor plan
9 access route
10 bathroom
11 hall
12 bedroom

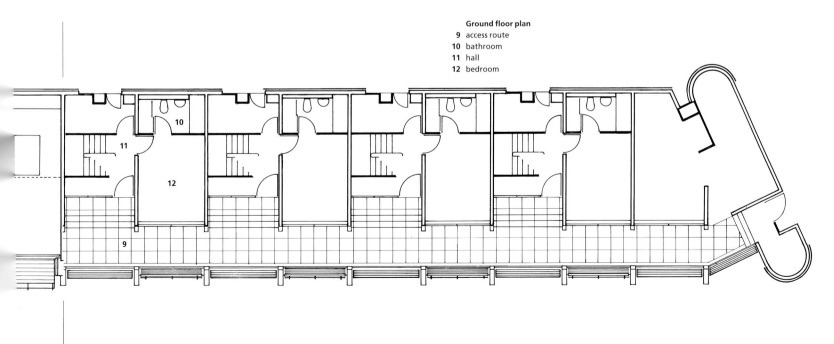

Houses at Grand Union Walk

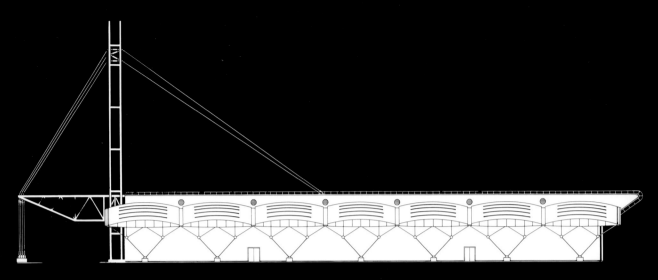

Homebase Store, Brentford, 1987

'The client recognized that this was an
important corner site with a very large
catchment area and that the standard
portal-framed metal-clad solution that
had been developed over the years for DIY
centres would not be appropriate on this
main route out of London.

   'Our solution, as with the Oxford Ice Rink,
was to use the structure to create a dramatic
image for the building. A tower was to carry
the Homebase logo in the same way as the
Gillette building opposite. It gave support
by means of steel tension rods to a massive
trussed girder which enabled the entire
4,246m² space to be free of columns. The rods
led to the ground in front of the building in a
very dramatic way somehow willing you to
understand that the load in them was the
same as the weight of 30 London buses. The
side of the building exposed a series of elegant
wing tips which reflect the curved and sloping
roofs each side of the spine.

   'A great deal of design work went into
this building and it is certainly intensively
used. The design team believe that at least
some of the visitors come because of the
architecture.' **NG**

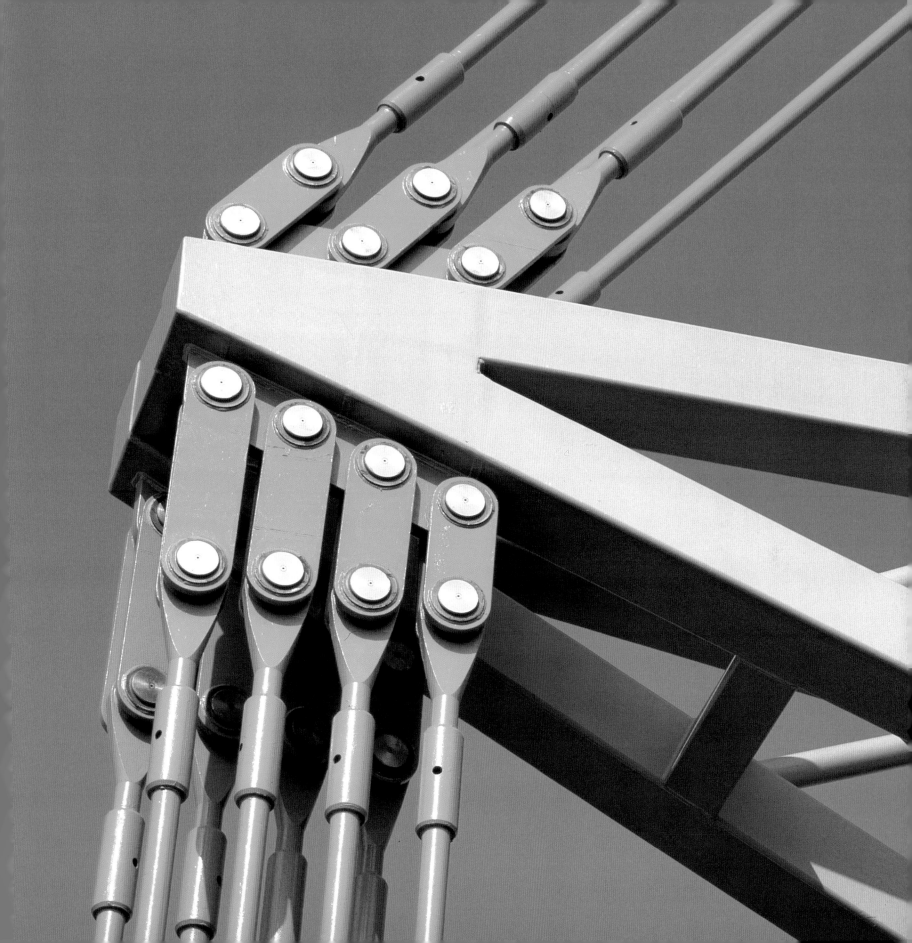

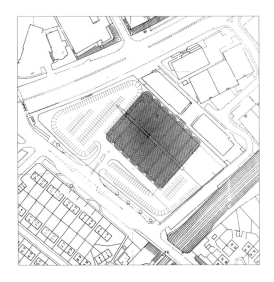

Site plan.

Previous page
Detail of the connection
between the tension rods and
the end of the spine beam.

Oblique view of the building.
The tower can be seen from a
considerable distance in both
directions along the A4.

214

The client for this project asked for a flagship trading store on the route to Heathrow Airport where there is considerable competition from other commercial landmarks. The brief insisted upon a low budget, but also a striking building. The company had a history of simple and inexpensive buildings, of a higher standard than most but still typical of the DIY warehouse/superstore. Inspired by the neighbouring factory towers (for example, the Gillette building designed by Bannister Fletcher) and taking a direction from the proximity to the airport, the architects devised a tall tower for signage and a radiused roof that is reminiscent of aerofoil plane wings. These also happily excluded any possibility of a flat roof – something that the client was anxious to avoid. The commercial needs were simple – over 4,000m² of column-free enclosed

Early sketch models exploring
different structural solutions
for the spine beam.

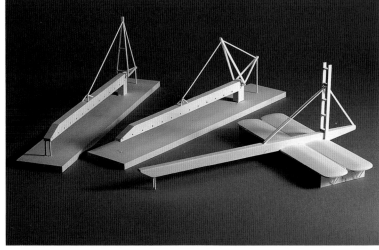

Nick Grimshaw's original
sketch showing how he
envisaged a spine beam
supported from a tower.

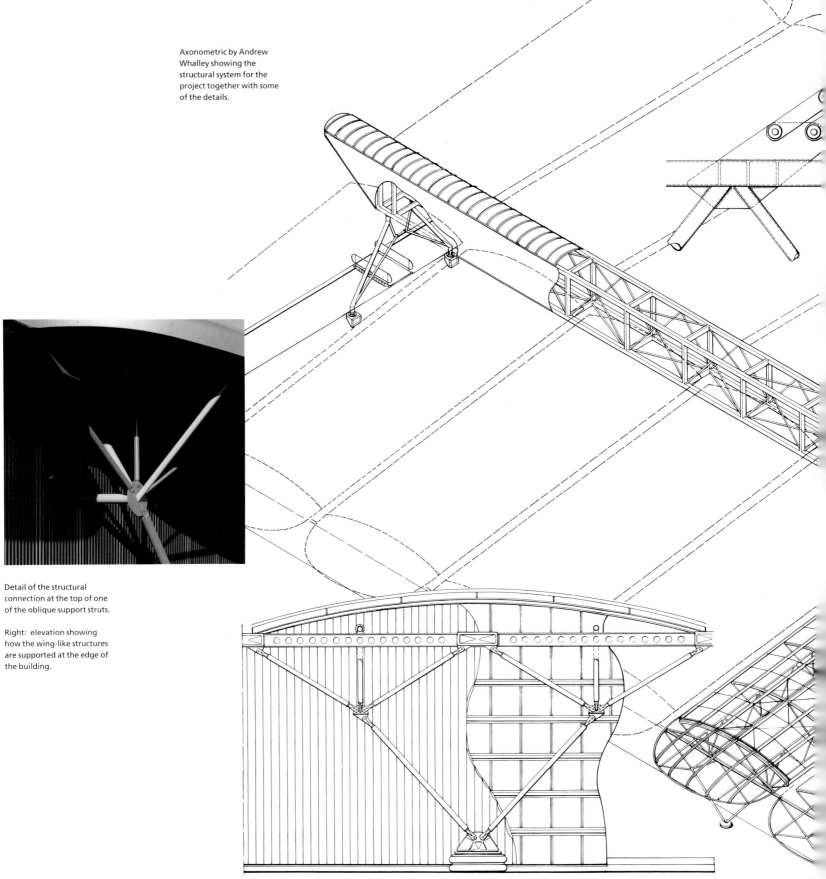

Axonometric by Andrew
Whalley showing the
structural system for the
project together with some
of the details.

Detail of the structural
connection at the top of one
of the oblique support struts.

Right: elevation showing
how the wing-like structures
are supported at the edge of
the building.

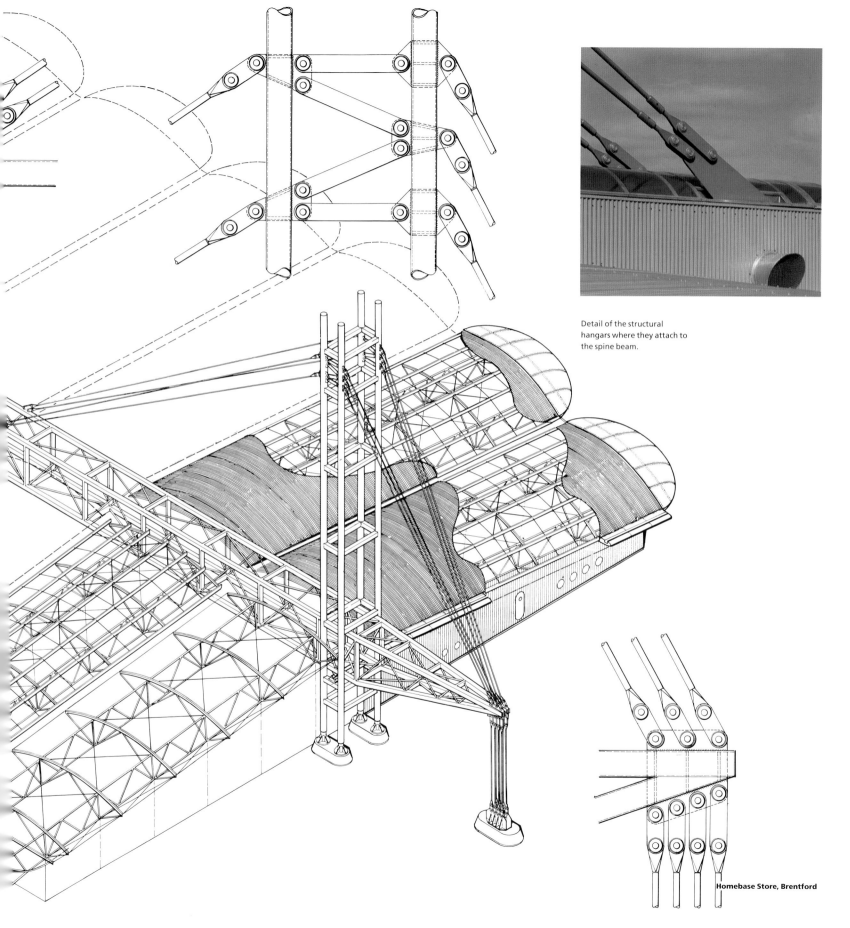

Detail of the structural
hangars where they attach to
the spine beam.

Homebase Store, Brentford

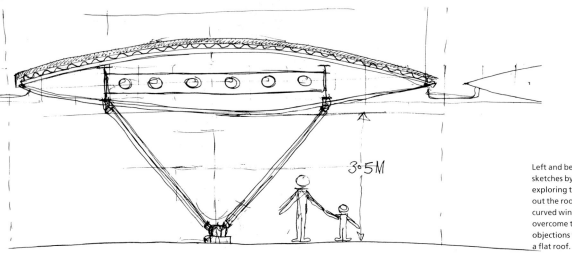

Part of the west elevation showing how the 'wing-tips' were formed in grp. The use of these mouldings allowed compound curves to be formed which were not feasible in ribbed metal.

3.5M

Left and below: original sketches by Nick Grimshaw exploring the idea of carrying out the roof in the form of curved wings in order to overcome the client's objections to having a flat roof.

space and as many car parking spaces on a level site as possible.

The structural principle is that of a tubular steel mast supporting a major trussed girder. The mast is the landmark tower and the enclosed beam forms what might be referred to as the 'fuselage'.

The tower and spine beam were delivered in sections and assembled and welded on site. The tower rests on concrete plinths and rises to 35m. The spine beam, which is some 70m in length and weighs about 80 tonnes, is threaded at one end through the lower section of the tower and rests at the other end on an A-frame trestle. Four 80mm diameter rods run from near the top of the tower to the mid-point of the beam to prevent any excessive deflection. Tie rods also restrain the stub end of the 'fuselage'. The seven arched space-

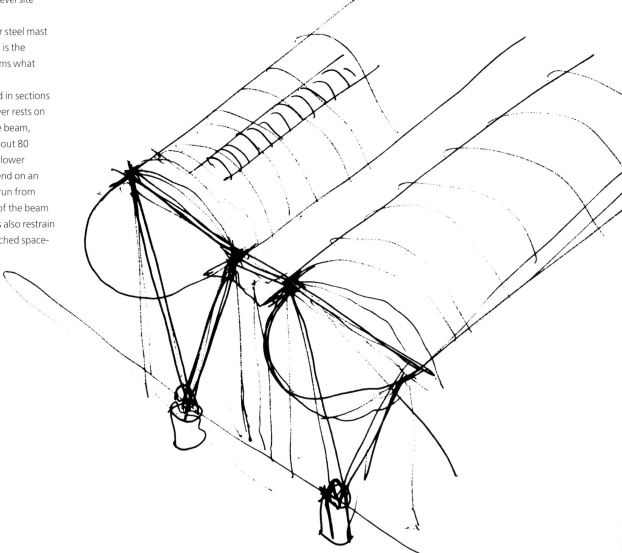

Detail showing tail end of the central spine.

frames that are the skeletons of the 'wing' roofs are supported at their tips by steel trestles around the perimeter of the building. The wings and wall cladding are constructed of two layers of aluminium which sandwich the insulation. The aluminium sheeting was supplied with a special sinusoidal profile to enhance its rigidity.

It is the 100m-long box girder that forms the main spine of the building and creates the clear internal span of 72m. It also houses an elegantly detailed roof-light which allows a great slice of light to penetrate the interior.

The deck to the south of the store was used for the sale of plants and other material that needed to be kept outdoors.

Plan of roof structure
showing central box girder
spine with 14 wing sections
spanning out to perimeter
supports.

222

0   10m

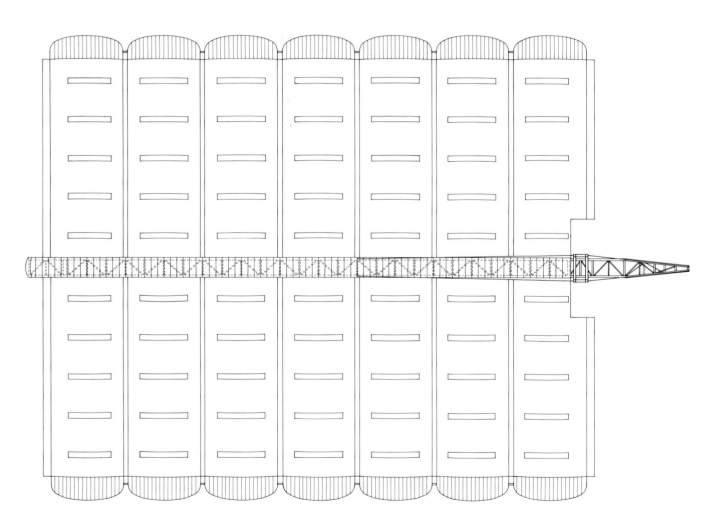

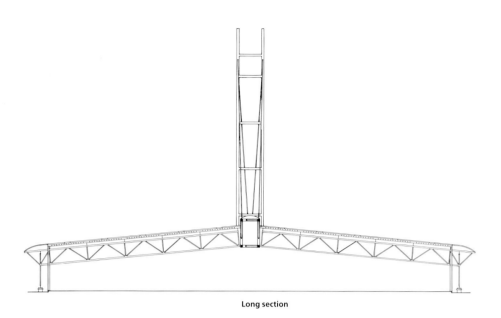

Long section

West elevation

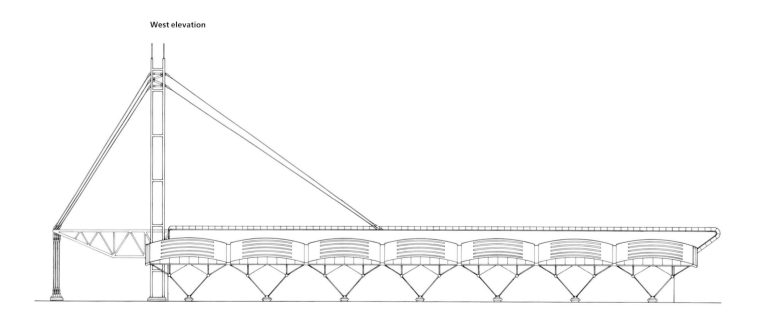

Homebase Store, Brentford

Financial Times Printing Works,
London Docklands, 1987–88

'Nearly all the newspapers had moved out
of Fleet Street to industrial sites, and the
Financial Times had decided to move from its
famous headquarters at Bracken House. They
had secured a key site in the Docklands but the
Dockland Architects wanted something more
than just a printing plant in a brick enclosure.

'We studied the printing process visiting
other printing works, and were astounded by
the scale and beauty of the presses which were
like great ship's engines and felt they should
be seen by the outside world. We developed a
structural system where the columns stretched
out arms to support 2m² sheets of glass,
creating a transparent facade 16m high and
96m long.

'The paper store and loading bay were
enclosed in vacuum-formed profiled
aluminium panels creating two solid ends
to the building. The Docklands Development
Board were delighted.

'The whole composition meant that the
workforce could have contact with the
outside world and the home-going
commuters had their journey enlivened by
seeing pink paper flashing through the

226   This is one of London's great buildings, developed as
a result of the regeneration of the Docklands that took
place in the 1980s. The client, the *Financial Times*, has
had a reputation as a good patron of architecture since
it commissioned an important headquarters building,
Bracken House almost next door to St Paul's Cathedral,
in the late 1950s from the then president of the Royal
Academy, Sir Albert Richardson. It was the sale of this
listed building and the relocation of the printing works
and the editorial offices on two different sites, that
resulted in the commissioning of this new printing
works on a site in the former East India Dock. The
Financial Times also organizes its own prestigious
architecture award, and so felt a special responsibility
to commission a good building, and one that would
markedly improve the working conditions of those
engaged in the printing process.

   The client had already purchased two large
state-of-the-art printing presses, each one 12m high
and over 35m long, which had to be accommodated
in the new printing hall. Grimshaw's work for Herman
Miller and other demanding clients had shown that
here was a practice in tune, not just with the new
technology, but also with the new industrial democracy

View of south elevation.

View of the entrance and two
of the service towers which
enclosed the emergency
staircases and other ancillary
functions.

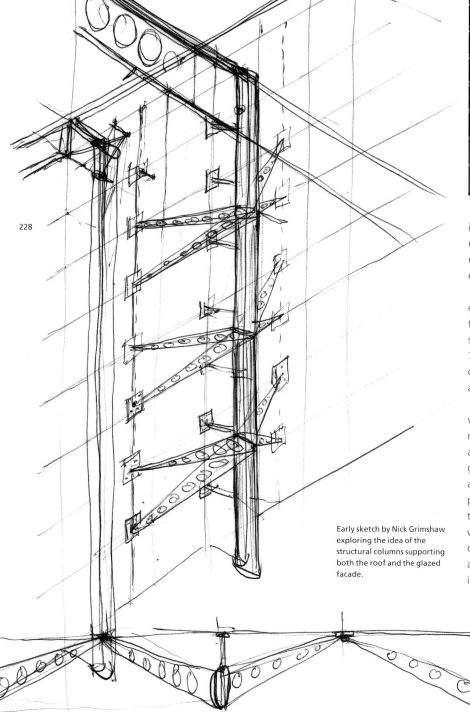

Early sketch by Nick Grimshaw
exploring the idea of the
structural columns supporting
both the roof and the glazed
facade.

in the workplace. The tight timetable of the
newspaper's uninterruptable production schedule
meant that the whole project had to be completed
exactly one year from the first briefing session.

The client was used to tight deadlines: in the context
of newspaper production one year seemed long enough
for the erection of a new printing works. The need for
speed could easily have encouraged even the *Financial
Times* and the architect to have opted for some simple
off-the-peg solution that would have been without
architectural distinction.

Instead, both client and architect, aware that they
were representing a prestigious international
newspaper, seem to have been motivated by speed
and determined to build a worthwhile building. The
giant presses are almost like pieces of high-tech
architecture themselves; their scale inspired the giant
press hall and encouraged the architects to celebrate
their operation by making them visible to the outside
world through a continuous glass wall. Once the
decision had been taken to give the building
a transparent heart, the more solid limbs fell naturally
into place. At one end, the rolls of pink newsprint are

Close up view of north
elevation showing how the
structural arms attached to
the column take lateral wind
forces. The glass is hung by
means of vertical tension rods
which are led back to the top
of the columns.

Architecture, Industry and Innovation

Detail of the facade.

Sketches by Nick Grimshaw
showing how tolerances in
x, y and z axes had to be taken
into account.

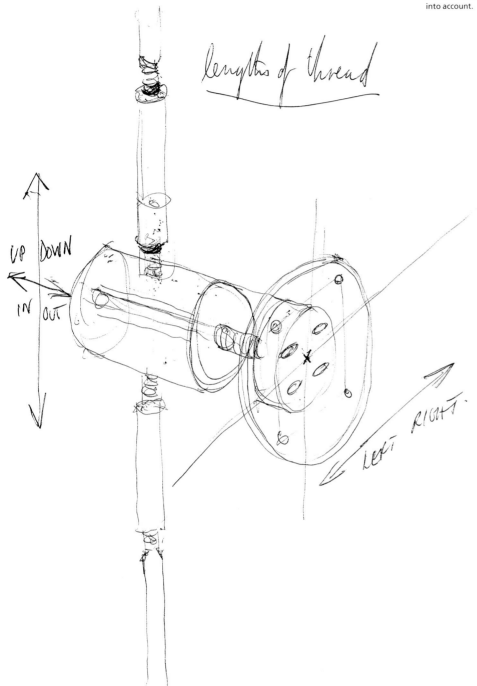

lengths of thread

UP DOWN

IN OUT

LEFT RIGHT.

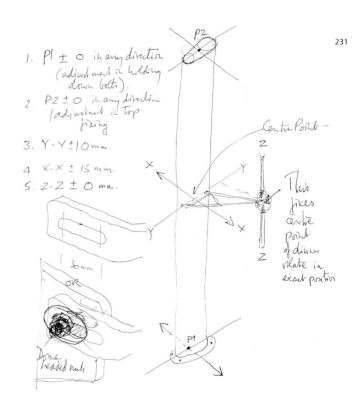

P2

1. P1 ± O in any direction
   (adjustment in holding
   down bolts).

2. P2 ± O in any direction
   (adjustment in top
   fixing

3. Y - Y ± 10 mm.

4. X - X ± 15 mm.

5. Z - Z ± O mm.

Centre Point

This
fixes
centre
point
of dinner
plate in
exact position

30 mm

OR

Dome
headed nuts

P1

Section through central stair
tower and southern glazed
wall.

Oblique view of south
elevation.

232

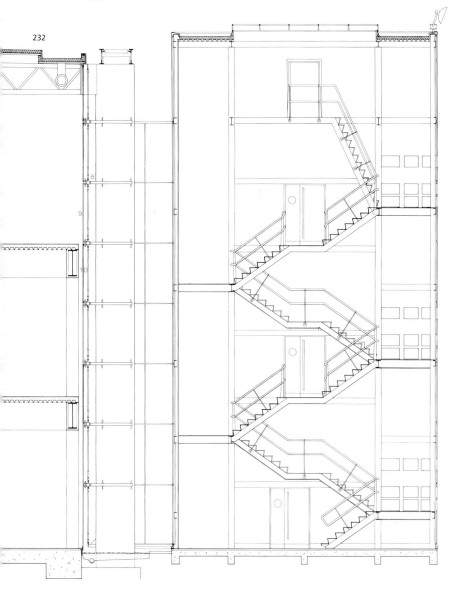

stored while, at the other, the dispatch department is housed; in between is the visible drama of the printing. The minimalist glass skin is the building's great triumph. It is 96m long by 16m high, formed of 2m² panes of 12mm toughened glass bolted at each corner and sealed with silicon. Drivers making for the nearby Blackwall Tunnel, and passers-by on the East India Dock Road, have one of the most dramatic views of the new printing technology at work to be found anywhere in the world. The great window is supported by an elegantly designed structure. Fabricated steel aerofoil columns at 6m centres support the roof and the considerable expanse and weight of glass. Each column has projecting steel cantilevers on either side which position the circular stainless steel plates that are bolted through the glass at each four-pane intersection.

View of the north facade as
seen by home-going
commuters. The pink paper
associated with the *Financial
Times* can be seen as it races
through the presses.

234

Nick Grimshaw on a visit to
see the presses rolling.

Oblique view showing the
inside of the north facade and
the vast scale of the printing
presses. Views out of the
building have certainly
improved working conditions.

Right: the complex
distribution system
transporting the papers from
the press to the inserting and
packaging areas.

The vertical load at the plates is taken by tension rods
extending upwards to the head of the column.

It was important for the building to have a dust-free
environment and to leave the interior working area
as open as possible. The innovative external structure
has made this possible, gaining working space for
the interior and simplifying the building's air-
conditioning requirements.

The entrance to the printing works is on the south
side where the staircase and lift are marked by two
partly-glazed towers. Two additional staircases are
located in separate curved aluminium-clad towers at
either end of the building. These are in the tradition of
Grimshaw's buildings where the service elements are
often housed in distinct, semi-detached towers, to
allow for a completely flexible main space.

The Financial Times Printing Works is a triumphant
demonstration of the made-to-measure high-tech
building that can be built speedily but with a clear
architectural style, while using all the advantages of
the industrialized building process.

237

Detail of the facade showing
the panels which were
vacuum formed from
Superplastic aluminium and
then factory coated with a
long-lasting paint system.

Below and right: detailed
cross section and elevation;
detailed vertical section
showing a panel joint.

238

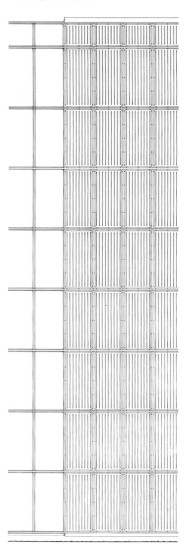

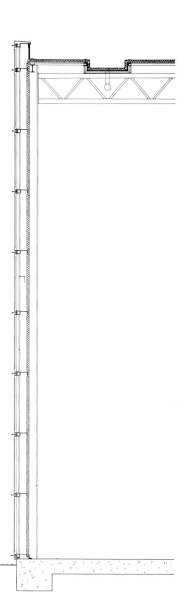

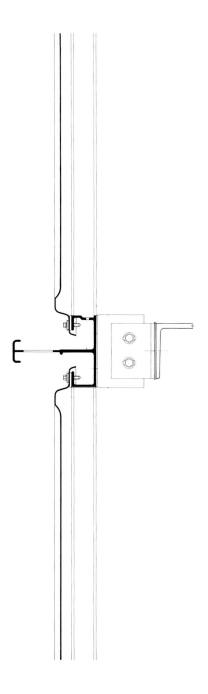

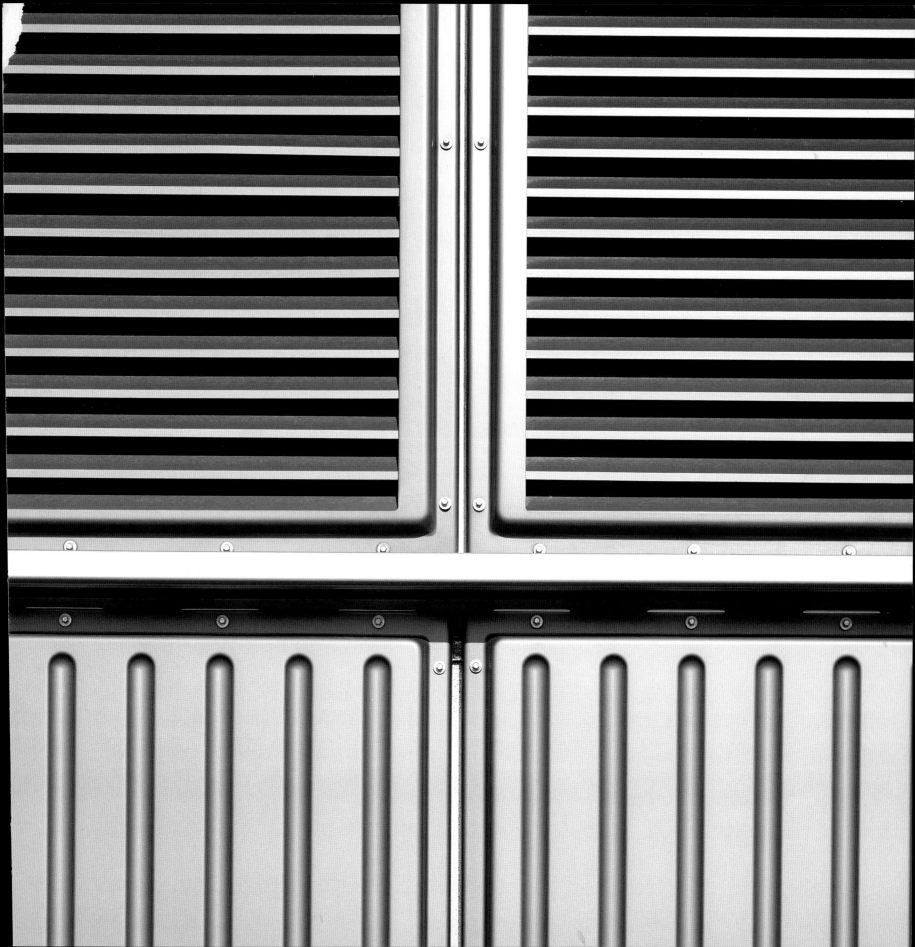

Previous page
North facade of the building
at dusk.

**North-south section through
production floors and
press hall**
1 car park
2 entrance and staircase
  tower
3 office space
4 plate making and
  composing room
5 publishing room
6 spine plant room
7 press hall

0   20m

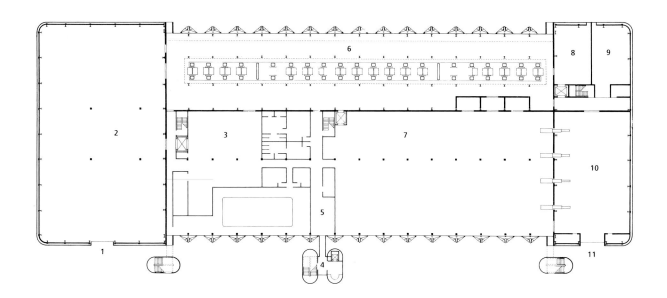

Ground floor plan
1 paper reel delivery
2 paper storage
3 workshops
4 entrance and security
  control desk
5 reception
6 press hall
7 publishing room
8 plant room
9 ink store
10 despatch bay
11 delivery trucks out

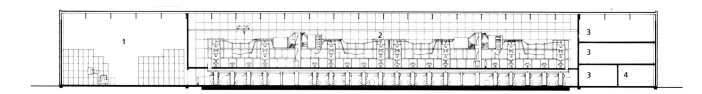

**East-west section
through press hall**
1 paper storage
2 press hall
3 plant rooms
4 ink store

Architecture, Industry and Innovation

Roof plan

1. underground water supply tank for sprinkler system
2. paper reel delivery
3. spine plant room
4. main entrance
5. car park
6. chiller plant
7. glass cleaning cradle
8. boiler flues
9. Financial Times Index signboard
10. gas meters and electricity board supply
11. smoke vents
12. despatch bay
13. vehicular entrance gates

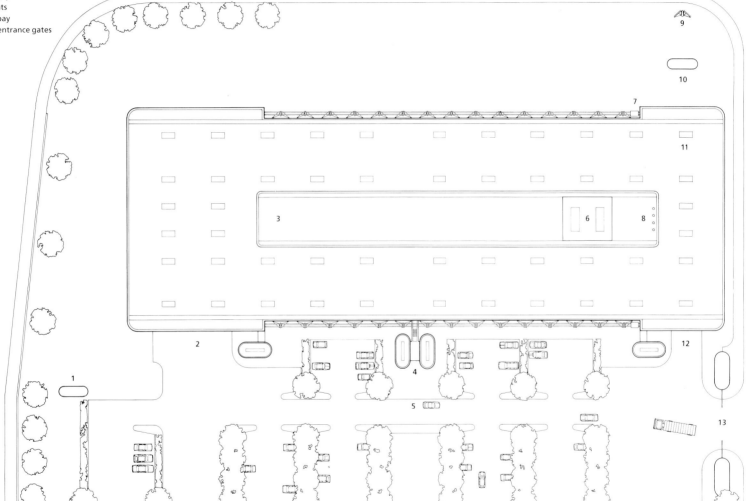

243

244 **Interview**

Transcript of an interview with Nicholas Grimshaw by
Jonathan Glancey, broadcast on BBC Radio 3 at 6.30pm on
2nd June 1989

JG *Engineering runs in Nicholas Grimshaw's veins. His
father was an aeronautic engineer and his great-grandfather,
Sir George Alderson, a well-known Victorian engineer, built
dams across the Nile. He has recently completed the dramatic
new steel and glass printing works for the Financial Times on
the Isle of Dogs and a supermarket that looks nothing like a
conventional supermarket for Sainsbury's in Camden Town.
His work has included the British headquarters for BMW cars,
the public ice rink in Oxford and numerous factories at home
and abroad. He's currently working on the design of the new
Channel Tunnel terminal at Waterloo, a project that he hopes
will restore lost glamour to British Rail. His work is often
described as 'high tech', a label that means little in itself but
which conjures up an architecture more concerned with
experimental structures of steel and glass, rather than
pediments, columns and traditional materials, and one that's
very near to engineering. Nick Grimshaw, how would you
define the difference between architecture and engineering?*

NG I think that all good architecture probably has a firm
structural base. People can look at buildings and understand
how they stay up and have a certain belief in them before
they start appreciating the spaces and the materials that the
buildings are made out of. From very early days I think that's
been the case; people understand arches, they understand
the structure of, say, a Gothic cathedral when they go into it
by looking at the buttresses on the outside.

JG *But is there a difference between a structure that's quite
clearly decorated, like a Gothic cathedral or something like
Tower Bridge, which seem to be clearly architectural; whilst
an engineering structure is often simple, expressing its
structure – don't you think there's quite clearly a big
difference between the two?*

NG I don't know. I think the Forth Railway Bridge is probably
a better example of a real engineering feat which actually
looks beautiful and is widely admired. I think there is
something slightly 'toytown' about Tower Bridge, partly
because you see it so often in children's collections of toys
and Meccano sets, but there are some marvellous
engineering details on it. The way the catenaries come down
very close to the road and you can see the actual joints and
the castings, it is a marvellous thing to look at.

JG *And did you play with Meccano sets when you were
a boy?*

NG Yes, I was very keen on Meccano. I think the interesting
thing about it was that you basically started with a set of
components in their barest form – nuts and bolts and strips of
metal with holes in them and so on – and you could invent
your own structures.

JG *What made you choose architecture? Quite clearly you
were fascinated by engineering from childhood and you had
a family background in engineering.*

NG Engineering is a terrific discipline and it's a mathematical
discipline. The engineer resolves problems, but he doesn't
have the same creative input that the architect does. The best
buildings are when really good architecture and good
engineering are combined. You don't get good architecture
with engineers alone, on the whole.

JG *Can you give an example, I mean an historic example of a
perfect marriage between architecture and engineering?*

NG Well, that's very difficult to do because nearly always one
thing is slightly more predominant than the other. Perhaps I

Architecture, Industry and Innovation

would go back to something like the Crystal Palace, which had neither an architect nor an engineer but actually is a perfect combination of the two, I think. It's a very systemized, beautifully thought-out structure which, in fact, had enormous architectural qualities about it.

JG *But the buildings you like, historically and today, and the buildings you build are all in, or largely in, steel and glass, and I wonder if you've got some engineer's bias against traditional architectural materials, such as bricks and mortar?*

NG Well I wouldn't say that at all. I'm a great admirer of Victorian brickwork and even perhaps more so of Edwardian brickwork, which I think is almost the ultimate kind of system building. The problem we have now is that the construction industry is not up to building like that. With cavity walls and so on, brickwork just isn't done in that solid form any more. What you're getting is a sort of evocation of the past, hoping somehow to call back the feeling with which the brickwork was done at Hampton Court, but actually not getting it at all.

JG *But lots of the buildings in high-tech style today, or certainly in the last 15 years or so, have often failed as a result of the use of new materials. I can think of the History Library at Cambridge or the Sainsbury's Centre at the University of East Anglia and, not to be cruel about them, they haven't lasted very long. Do you see buildings lasting as long as Victorian ones if they're built in new materials?*

NG On the whole those buildings that have failed in recent years have not failed because of the materials used, they've failed because of the detailing. It's a question of the way the buildings are put together and how much people care for the buildings. All buildings have to be maintained. If you go past Westminster Abbey you'll see scaffolding almost constantly

up there where they're piecing together stonework. The same thing with the Houses of Parliament. They've been round and round it several times in my lifetime trying to keep it up. So I think it's a complete myth that brick or stone buildings last forever. I think a building will last as long as people want it to last.

JG *But do people take unnecessary risks? If we go back to your ice rink at Oxford, you've got a very large roof held up by these very dramatic tall masts which have wires stretching from them to support the roof. Is that an exaggerated structure and is it one that could lead to unnecessary problems?*

NG Well, an ice rink is a special kind of place, it's an entertainment building. I would like to feel that ice-skating was a perpetual kind of thrill for the human being, but it may not be and the building may turn to different uses in the future. As an enclosure I see no reason why it shouldn't last indefinitely if it's looked after. What you call wires are actually quite thick stainless steel rods and we went to great lengths to make sure that the pieces of the building which are exposed are easily maintainable. Those that aren't, like those rods, are stainless steel so that they don't need maintenance. It's very easy to paint the masts and, of course with North Sea oil rig finishes, steelwork can be protected for up to ten to 15 years before it needs painting again. So the general technology of protecting steelwork is very much more advanced than when the earlier steel structures were put up. I would say steel is a very good long-lasting material to use now. The walls of that building were, rather appropriately I thought, in panels which have been widely used throughout Europe for cold storage buildings. They're an absolutely standard product, and if any of them started to be defective they could be replaced extremely easily. In principle, it's a

building which will last as long as people love it.

JG *I wonder about the look of the thing. I mean this building we're talking about is in Oxford, which is the city of honey-coloured stone. Your building, built of the refrigerator panels, is grey and steely and some people might be quite concerned that it borrows from refrigerating systems. Do you think the aesthetics of a building like that can actually fit in to an historic town?*

NG Well look, it's on the site where they traditionally have fairs in Oxford, on the recreation ground, and they still have circuses beside it. So I think everyone quite expected a building with some kind of strong image and interest and joy and life about it. They weren't looking for a monument but they were looking for a building which attracted people. You know, it has got a glazed wall right across the north end which is fortuitous in that you don't get any sun in there, but it does mean that people can see right across the ice going past in their cars or walking past the building. The local paper referred to it as 'The Cutty Sark'. The fact that it's got the exposed structure and the two masts, one each end, does give it a very, very strong image, but that was really precisely part of our brief. The town councillors wanted a building which would be noticed, which would attract the young people of Oxford – and it does. There are five or six hundred people in there often, and one really nice thing I heard from the City Engineer of Oxford was that vandalism and graffiti in the town has gone down very dramatically since we built the ice rink. It's become a social focus centre and it's a place where young people can congregate and talk. So I think that basically a building like that will last as long as it has a social function, and as long as people like it. If it outlives its function, well, it will probably be replaced by another building.

246

JG *There's a current architectural trend which is to get buildings to fit into towns, which often means aping traditional styles or using the same sort of materials; I wonder, are your buildings designed to shock us out of that way of thinking?*

NG As I said earlier on, I think that 'aping' the past is not the way of 'fitting in', basically. Fitting in is to do with things like scale and height, light and shade, the feeling that a building has a ground level at people level and that sort of thing. It's not to do with just matching the building next door. Good architects in the past have never done that; they've always tried to build in the best way they could at the time. Taking the building you mentioned, the Sainsbury's scheme at Camden Town, 'fitting in' was a critical issue there because we were trying very, very hard to blend in with the townscape. There was a row of Georgian houses facing the building site. The building that was there before was a slightly ungainly bread factory (the ABC Bakery) well-known to everybody. This was a mixture of styles and a very big, bulky building, rather out of scale with what was there. One of the ironic things was that certain preservation-minded old fogeys in Camden Town thought that the building should stay simply out of unbridled nostalgia, not because it fitted in or even because it was particularly nice, just because it was there. You have to have a certain amount of sympathy. So often when you see a new building going up these days, or rather when you see an old building coming down, you tend to assume that the new building is going to be worse than whatever was there before. However, in this case the building has been quite widely accepted by the people that live in Camden Town as fitting in relatively well with its surroundings.

JG *But it's also been said that the building is quite grey – on*

a dull, dark, cloudy day it can look rather too steely – whilst bricks still have a sort of warmth on the other side of the road in bad weather. Why do you never use colour?*

NG We have used colour a lot in our buildings and are known for doing colourful buildings, particularly with industrial buildings, and in some cases even causing a certain amount of stirring up in the neighbourhood. In this case, we actually started off with a very bright blue colour to the panels. However, in the end, and going back to our earlier discussion about how long will buildings last, I thought a bright colour in this street setting wouldn't have been right; I think it might have become dated. I see that building – which is very carefully detailed and well built – lasting a long time in the street scene. I therefore thought muted colours were more appropriate. Actually, the sun's very low at this time of the year, but when it gets higher in summer you'll see that in fact there are about four different greys and blues on the building, not to mention the stainless steel, so it isn't all one colour. You'll notice that it's actually quite subtle and built to express the materials it's made of, not relying on artificial colour which might date.

JG *It's curious you should talk about that building as being one that will last for a long time; and I'm not questioning its structural validity or anything, but it seems that retailing changes very, very fast – won't that building go out of date just like any shopping mall or modern shopping centre?*

NG This might perhaps bring us back to structure, because the structure there is very simple. It's an arched structure, which is quite a big departure for Sainsbury's. We set out to create this market hall feel with an arched structure spanning 43 metres; this is quite a wide span. It is a structure which is understandable by people walking past the building. They

can see how it works. They can see the columns which support one side of the span. They can see the tie rods which counterbalance the beams. The structure is exposed in a fairly grand way and I would say that the building has a strength and a lasting quality. So if retailing is no longer the thing to do on that street corner, then the building will last and it can be used for many other purposes.

JG *Now you talk quite a lot about flexibility and in fact, many years ago now, you built a building in Bath for Herman Miller and I think you described that plan as an 'indeterminate' building. I wonder if you could tell us a little about that indeterminacy, about how buildings can change their use?*

NG Again, it takes me back to this question of buildings being liked by their users. The thing at Herman Miller was that we started off with a complete furniture factory all under one roof. Raw materials – that is, chipboard and timber etc – cardboard boxes for packing the goods, machinery for making the furniture, and so on – everything under one roof. And gradually, as they expanded, they had to move out a lot of the storage functions and bring in new manufacturing processes. So what went on in the building ebbed and flowed, and we wanted to put up a building which was capable of accepting all that ebb and flow. We therefore devised a very carefully organized servicing system and structure. Even the external panels were capable of being changed for glass. The whole skin of the building could be changed and, over the last ten years or so, it has changed dramatically in external appearance. It really does reflect the wishes of the people working in it and it is fascinating going back there, as I do quite often, to see the building. The people really like it. They talk to me and they're the same people that were in there when it was first built.

Architecture, Industry and Innovation

Apparently, it has one of the lowest turnovers of workforce of any building in the area.

JG *Now, that could be because it's just such a nice employer or they pay very well!*

NG I asked the same question myself and apparently they pay slightly less, so it must be something to do with the environment.

JG *I'm interested in this because I did do some homework and, as you know, the Lloyd's building by Richard Rogers is under a lot of criticism. It is going to be changed slightly inside. I also found out that your Financial Times building is very popular with the workforce and I wonder why it is that, although you are building in a style of architecture that other architects use, you seem to manage to get the people on your side. Is there some magic ingredient?*

NG I think it's perhaps to do with trying to keep the concept extremely clear and simple; to avoid unnecessary frills and complications in the buildings. I went past a DIY store the other day which was just corrugated metal cladding over a portal frame. The client obviously thought this looked a bit bald so he added trusses on the outside of the building, just to make it look more 'high tech'. I thought that was an extraordinary thing to do. I believe that people can see the difference; I think they realize these trusses are pure decoration, they're not really holding the building up. I hope, and I think it's true, that people can walk past the Financial Times Printing Works and they can see what's going on; they can see there are columns there, 50 feet high, which are holding up the glazed wall. It's one of the largest and longest glazed walls in London, I suspect, at over 300 feet long and 50 feet high.

JG *You're just about to build an even bigger building which is going to be the terminal for the Channel Tunnel at Waterloo. I wonder if you could tell us if that building is picking up on the same sort of aesthetic – will that be a big engineering building, and how can you make that popular?*

NG I like to feel that British Rail selected us as architects because of our great interest in engineering and detailing of large-scale structures. We had fairly recently done the Financial Times at that time, and I think they liked the look of it. They liked the way the structure was done, the way we'd handled steel, glass and aluminium. They knew they were looking for a wide-span, elegant structure which was going to be 400 metres long, a train hall in the real heroic tradition of Victorian railway stations. On the other hand, they have to bear in mind that the trains are going to be very sleek, 'high-tech', to use your word, pieces of technology. They are quiet, electric and are going to slip in there more like jet planes than noisy, smelly Victorian railway engines. So I think they were looking for a building that would reflect that and would also reflect the streamlined quality which they were after in terms of getting passengers through very quickly.

JG *But what will somebody see as they come running off the train and dashing through the barrier, this is the first time they've come to London perhaps; what will they see in your terminal?*

NG Well, I hope they will see beautifully detailed structure and admire it in the same way that they might admire Brunel's detailing of the roof at Paddington. I hope they'll feel they've really arrived somewhere. They'll see surfaces which are easy to clean and generally cared for, as there are in so many of our public buildings and airports. I hope that feeling will carry on through all the areas they have to go through.

JG *I suppose one could describe this building as a gateway to London. You seem to have built several such gateways; there's the Financial Times building in the East End, the Homebase store in the west, Camden Town in the north, now Waterloo in the south. Do you think you'll be remembered as an architect who created the new gateways for London?*

NG Well, I feel that people enjoy having markers on their route into town. I'm a great admirer of the Hoover building on the Great West Road and I think that people do recognize that as being an important marker on the way into London, a building which reflects the heroic days of industry and where real effort and attention was put into creating something. I hope people can see the difference still; I think they can. When the brick wall which is in front of the Financial Times comes down (as part of the road widening there), the facade will be exposed to view and I think anyone travelling up and down the East India Dock Road will feel they've passed something special. I hope they'll like the fact that you can see the press behind the glass whirring away printing the *Financial Times*; that you see the presses there, all beautifully clean and well-cared for, with very, very high technology equipment surrounding them. I think it's a great advertisement for the *Financial Times*, but it's also doing something for the people of London.

JG *Nick Grimshaw, thank you very much.*

Project data

* These projects were carried out during the time Nick Grimshaw
was in partnership with Terry Farrell in the practice entitled
Farrell/Grimshaw Partnership (FGP)

Service Tower, Student Hostel, London, 1967
Overall dimensions   25m high, 30 pods
Overall area   212m²
Structural dimensions   1.5m (plan dim) hexagonal steel pylon with
projecting steel arms supporting pods O/A 0.7m
Contract value   £250,000 approx
*FGP   Nick Grimshaw
Client   International Students Club (Church of England) Ltd
Structural Engineer   Ove Arup & Partners
Quantity Surveyor   Hanscomb Partnership

Apartments, 125 Park Road, London, 1968
Overall dimensions   17.3m x 17.3m x 30.5m high
Overall area   approx 3,300m²
Structural dimensions   central core 9.1m x 7.6m perimeter columns at
1.8m, 3.4m and 4m centres
Contract value   £230,000 approx
*FGP   Paul Gibson, Nick Grimshaw, Graham Saunders
Client   Mercury Housing Society Ltd
Structural Engineer   Anthony Hunt Associates
Quantity Surveyor   Hanscomb Partnership
Service Engineer   Peter Martin

Citroën Warehouse, Runnymede, 1972
Overall dimensions   113m x 67m
Overall area   7,710m² (warehouse), 930m² (office)
Structural dimensions   33m x 6.28m
Contract value   £510,140
*FGP   Nick Grimshaw, Brian Taggart
Client   McKay Securities plc
Structural Engineer   Peter Brett Associates
Quantity Surveyor   MDA: Monk & Dunstone, Mahon & Scears
Service Engineer   James R Briggs & Associates

Headquarters for Editions Van de Velde, Tours, France, 1975
Overall dimensions   25m x 35m
Overall area   875m²
Structural dimensions   5m x 10m grid
Contract value   £100,000 approx
*FGP   Nick Grimshaw, Jeff Scherer
Client   Editions Van de Velde
Structural Engineer   W E Budgeon & Partners
Quantity Surveyor   Hanscomb Partnership
Service Engineer   Ronald Hurst Associates

Factory for Herman Miller, Bath, 1976
Overall dimensions   90m x 60m
Overall area   6,320m²
Structural dimensions   10m x 20m
Contract value   £821,600
*FGP   Nick Grimshaw, Jeff Scherer
Client   Herman Miller Ltd
Structural Engineer   Peter Brett Associates
Quantity Surveyor   Hanscomb Partnership
Service Engineer   Ronald Hurst Associates

Advanced Factory Units, Winwick Quay, 1978
Overall dimensions   110m x 70m
Overall area   7,648m² (internal area)
Structural dimensions   grid of 10m x 17.5m with primary beams
at 10m centres
Contract value   £890,000
*FGP   Nick Grimshaw, David Nixon, Norman Partridge, Brian Taggart
Client   Warrington New Town Development Corporation
Structural Engineer   Warrington New Town Development
Corporation
Quantity Surveyor   Warrington New Town Development Corporation
Service Engineer   Warrington New Town Development Corporation

Headquarters for BMW, Bracknell, 1980
Overall dimensions   approx 30m x 60m
Overall area   15,950m²
Structural dimensions   grids: 10m x 20m, 10m x 10m, 10m x 5m
Contract value   £4m approx
*FGP   Nick Grimshaw, Brian Taggart, Mark Walker
Client   BMW (UK) Ltd
Structural Engineer   Peter Brett Associates
Services Engineer   Ronald Hurst Associates

Factory Units, Queen's Drive, Nottingham, 1980
Overall dimensions   40m x 265m
Overall area   14,058m²
Structural dimensions   20m x 10m
Contract value   £1.8m
*FGP   Nick Grimshaw, David Richmond, Brian Taggart
Client   Electricity Supply Nominees Ltd
Structural Engineer   Peter Brett Associates
Quantity Surveyor   Andrew & Boyd
Service Engineer   Ronald Hurst Associates

Sports Halls for IBM, Winchester, 1980
Overall dimensions   24m x 18m
Overall area   432m²
Structural dimensions   frame spans 18m at 5.25m centres
Contract value   £100,000 approx
*FGP   Simon Bean, Mark Goldstein, Nick Grimshaw, David Harriss
Client   IBM (UK) Ltd
Structural Engineer   Felix J Samuely & Partners
Quantity Surveyor   Michael F Edwards & Associates
Services Engineer   Ronald Hurst Associates

Furniture Factory for Vitra, Weil-am-Rhein, Germany, 1981
Overall dimensions   125m x 78m
Overall area   11,900m²
Structural dimensions   25m frame spans
Contract value   £2.5m approx
NGP   Zully Garcia, Nick Grimshaw, Eva Jiricna, Philip McLean,
Gunther Schnell
Client   Vitra GmbH
Structural Engineer   Management Contractor
Quantity Surveyor   Management Contractor

Wiltshire Radio Station, Wootton Bassett, 1982
Overall dimensions   14.5m x 11.75m
Overall area   170m²
Structural dimensions   14m x 11m
Contract value   £198,000 approx
NGP   Simon Bean, Don Gray, Nick Grimshaw
Client   Wiltshire Radio plc
Structural Engineer   Felix J Samuely & Partners
Quantity Surveyor   Hanscomb Partnership
Electrical Engineer   Yates Associates
Mechanical Engineer   Peter Horton Associates

Herman Miller Distribution Centre, Chippenham, 1982
Overall dimensions   74.4m x 93.6m
Overall area   6,970m²
Structural dimensions   width 28.8m x 36m x 28.8m
Contract value   £1,689,000
NGP   Mark Goldstein, Nick Grimshaw, Ian McArdie, Neven Sidor
Client   Herman Miller (UK) Ltd
Structural Engineer   Peter Brett Associates
Quantity Surveyor   Gardiner & Theobald
Services Engineer   YRM Engineers

Ice Rink, Oxford, 1984
Overall dimensions   72m x 38m
Overall area   3,506m²
Structural dimensions   72m clear span
Contract value   £1.85m
NGP   Nick Grimshaw, Kevin Jackson, Ian McArdle, Neven Sidor
Client   Oxford City Council
Structural Engineer   Ove Arup & Partners
Quantity Surveyor   Davis Belfield & Everest
Services Engineer   Ove Arup & Partners

Headquarters for Ladkarn, London Docklands, 1985
Overall dimensions   40.8m x 28.8m
Overall area   1,535m²
Structural dimensions   14.4m x 31.2m
Contract value   £650,000
NGP   Simon Bean, Nick Grimshaw, David Harriss, Matthew Keeler
Structural Engineer   Ove Arup & Partners
Quantity Surveyor   Ladkarn (Haulage) Ltd
Services Engineer   Ove Arup & Partners

Research Centre for Rank Xerox, Welwyn Garden City, 1988
Overall dimensions   30m x 42m
Overall area   4,140m²
Structural dimensions   12m x 6m
Contract value   £4.1m
NGP   Nick Grimshaw, David Harriss, Frank Ling, John Prevc,
Wolfgang Zimmer
Client   Xerox Research (UK) Ltd
Structural Engineer   Ove Arup & Partners
Quantity Surveyor   Davis Belfield & Everest
Services Engineer   Ove Arup & Partners

Leisure Centre, Stockbridge, 1986–88
Overall dimensions   44m x 36m
Overall area   2,468m²
Structural dimensions   20m clear span
Contract value   £3.6m
NGP   Mark Bryden, Christopher Campbell, Nick Grimshaw,
David Heeley, Christopher Nash
Client   Metropolitan Borough of Knowsley
Structural Engineer   Ove Arup & Partners
Quantity Surveyor   David Belfield & Everest
Services Engineer   Ove Arup & Partners

Superstore for Sainsbury's, London, 1986–88
Retail area   total area approx 6,000m²
Workshop   2,322m², **Crèche** 93m², **Car Park** 303 cars
Contract value   £14m
NGP   Sally Draper, Mark Fisher, Rowena Fuller, Nick Grimshaw,
Christine Humphreys, Christopher Nash, Gunter Schnell, Neven Sidor,
Hin Tan, Simon Templeton
Client   J Sainsbury plc
Structural Engineer   Kenchington Little & Partners
Quantity Surveyor   Henry Riley & Son Ltd
Mechanical & Electrical Engineer   J Sainsbury plc

Houses at Grand Union Walk, London, 1986–88
10 houses   single aspect, 3 storeys, 3 bedrooms, 2 bathrooms and
1 bed maisonette and 1 bed-sitting room flat
Structural dimensions   7.5m party wall to party wall
Contract value   included in overall contract sum of £14m for the
Superstore Development
NGP   Sally Draper, Nick Grimshaw, Neven Sidor
Client   J Sainsbury plc
Structural Engineer   Kenchington Little & Partners
Quantity Surveyor   Henry Riley & Son Ltd
Mechanical & Electrical Engineer   J Sainsbury plc

Homebase Store, Brentford, 1987
Overall dimensions   tower 35m 100m ridge beams, internal span 72m
Overall area   4,100m²
Structural dimensions   45m x 9m
Contract value   £2.6m
NGP   Rowena Fuller, Nick Grimshaw, David Harriss, David Heeley,
Andrew Whalley
Client   Homebase Ltd
Structural Engineer   Ernst Green Partnership Ltd
Quantity Surveyor   Basil Cohen & Partners

Financial Times Printing Works, London Docklands, 1987–88
Overall dimensions   144m x 52m
Overall area   14,000m²
Structural dimensions   12m spine x 18m bays
Contract value   £18.3m
NGP   Paul Grayshon, Nick Grimshaw, Douglas Keys, Rosemary Latter,
Frank Ling, Christoper Nash, Wolfgang Zimmer
Client   The Financial Times
Structural Engineer   J Robinson & Son Ltd
Press/Interior Architect   Robinson Design Partnership
Services Engineer   Cundall Johnson & Partners Ltd
Management Contractor   Bovis Construction Ltd

Awards
for projects included in this volume

Royal Institute of British Architects

1975   Citroën Warehouse, Runnymede (Commendation)
1978   Factory for Herman Miller, Bath (Principal Award)
1980   Advanced Factory Units, Winwick Quay (Principal Award)
1980   Headquarters for BMW, Bracknell (Commendation)
1983   Factory Units, Queen's Drive, Nottingham (Commendation)
1986   Herman Miller Distribution Centre, Chippenham
         (Commendation)
1989   Financial Times Printing Works (National and Regional Awards)
1990   Research Centre for Rank Xerox (Regional Award)
1991   Leisure Centre, Stockbridge (Regional Award)

Financial Times Industrial Architecture Awards

1977   Factory for Herman Miller, Bath (Principal Award)
1980   Advanced Factory Units, Winwick Quay (Commendation)

Structural Steel Design Awards

1969   Service Tower, Student Hostel, London
         (Principal Award)
1977   Factory for Herman Miller, Bath (Principal Award)
1989   Financial Times Printing Works (Commendation)
1989   Homebase Store, Brentford (Commendation)

Civic Trust Awards

1978   Factory for Herman Miller, Bath (Commendation)
1982   Sports Hall for IBM, Winchester (Commendation)
1989   Financial Times Printing Works (National and Regional Awards)
1990   Research Centre for Rank Xerox (Commendation)
1991   Leisure Centre, Stockbridge (Commendation)

Department of the Environment Awards

1973   Apartments, 125 Park Road, London (Commendation)

British Construction Industry Awards

1988   Homebase Store, Brentford (High Commendation)
1989   Financial Times Printing Works (High Commendation)

Royal Fine Art Commission /
Sunday Times Building of the Year Award

1989   Financial Times Printing Works (Joint Winner)

Other Awards

1977   Business and Industry Awards: Factory for Herman Miller, Bath
         (Certificate of Merit)
1980   Ambrose Congreve Award for Architecture:
         Headquarters for BMW, Bracknell (Commendation)
1981   European Award for Steel Structures:
         Headquarters for BMW Bracknell (Commendation)
1987   BSC Structural Steel Classics 1906–86:
         Factory for Herman Miller, Bath
1989   Illustrated London News Award:
         Financial Times Printing Works (Winner –
         Development Category)
1990   European Award for Industrial Architecture:
         Financial Times Printing Works (Second Prize)
1990   BBC Design Awards:
         Financial Times Printing Works (Finalist)
1995   AJ Centenary Medal for Contribution to Architecture

Bibliography

For projects completed during the period 1967–88

General

Archetype   May 1974: Journal of Environmental Technology, RMIT: 'Anti-Formalism in Contemporary British Architecture', N Ross Ramus

Archigram   1965: 'Newcomer, Nick Grimshaw' (student thesis)

Architects' Journal   27 March 1974: 'Architects' Approach to Architecture: Architecture and Pragmatism – Farrell/Grimshaw talk at RIBA', Alistair Best

Architects' Journal   17 August 1977: 'Garden Triangles'

Architects' Journal   21 July 1982: 'International Garden Festival Exhibition Competition Scheme'

Architects' Journal   30 March 1995: 'Grimshaw Triumphs in first RIBA Competitive Interview'

Architects' Journal Centenary Issue   9 March 1995: 'Architecture: The 70s, 80s, 90s'

Architectural Design   February 1973: 'Farrell/Grimshaw: Recent Work'

Architectural Design   May 1974: Pick of the Projects (Project Awards), Millman Street redevelopment

Architectural Design   May 1976: 'Farrell-Grimshaw', James Meller

Architectural Review   December 1993: Products Survey

Architecture et Industrie   ('Passé et avenir d'un mariage de raison') Centre de Création Industrielle, Centre Georges Pompidou, 1983

Architettura Urbanistia Controspazio   January 1994: 'Struttura, spazio, pelle: La ricerca del "cristallino" di Nicholas Grimshaw', Cristina Donati

Arquitectura Viva   March/April 1994: 'Libros – Hopkins y Grimshaw: Opciones del High-Tec'

Blueprint   February 1985: 'Urbane Spaceman', Martin Pawley

Blueprint   March 1988: 'The Impeccable Logic of Nick Grimshaw', Rick Poynor

British Architecture Today   Six Protagonists, Electa Milan (5th Venice Biennale), 1991

Building   22 April 1977: 'Matching Talents', Gontran Goulden

Building   23 July 1982: 'High Tech with Zip', Colin Davies

Building   15 January 1988: 'Flight Path to Fame', Sutherland Lyall

Building   29 January 1988: 'Grimshaw Produces a Model Exhibition', Sutherland Lyall

Building Design   25 February 1972: 'The Men Most Likely to…' Louis Wilkins

Building Design   15 September 1972: 'Action Replan'

Building Design   15 September 1978: 'Industrial Patchwork', Jack Christopher

Building Design   22 January 1988: 'Keeping the faith', Colin Davies

Building Design   Supplement, March 1990: Special Report on Cladding , 'Allowing Function to Dictate Form' (David Harriss' Lecture to the Building Industry Trust)

Building Design   20th Anniversary Supplement, 1990

Building Design   30 March 1990: 'Floating Voters'

Building Design   12 November 1993: 'Seven Day Mission to Make it in Japan', José Manser

Building Design   3 February 1995: 'Comparisons of the Year', Kester Rattenbury

Chartered Quantity Surveyor   September 1982: 'A New Setting for British Industry', Guy Morton Smith, Brian Taggart, Joe Burns

Contemporary European Architects 2   Dirk Meyhofer, Benedikt Taschen, Cologne: 1993

Design   October 1980: 'The Mobile Office', Deyan Sudjic

Deutsche Bauzeitung   December 1988: 'Die Schwelle zur Architektur', ('When Structure becomes Architecture'), Nick Grimshaw

Experimental Architecture   Peter Cook, Studio Vista: 1970

Financial Times   18 January 1988: 'Designs for Living', Colin Amery

Guardian   25 January 1988: 'The Hang of It', Martin Pawley (review of Exhibition at RIBA)

Herman Miller Ltd   'Understanding People's Needs at Work', Robert L Propst

ICA Model Futures   12 April–22 May 1983: Exhibition catalogue, Bob Allies, quotation from Nick Grimshaw's AA thesis

Industrialised Building   February 1968: Systems and Components, 'Students Furniture Unit'

Industrie Bauten Gestalten   Degenhard Sommer, Acus Verlag, Vienna: 1989

Industriebau die Vision der Lean Company Praxis Report, Degenhard Sommer, Birkhauser: 1993

Journal of the Royal Society of Arts   December 1984: 'The Future of Industrial Building', Nick Grimshaw

Journal of the Royal Society of Arts   September 1986: 'Re-inventing the Factory', RSA-Cubitt Trust Panel (summary of a seminar held on 22 October 1985)

Lieux? de Travail   Centre de Création Industrielle, Centre George Pompidou, 1986

London Architect   April 1995: 'Dealing with Capital Cost'

National Structural Steel Association   National Structural Steel Conference 1986 – 'The Changing World of Steel Construction'

New British Architecture   Jonathan Glancey, Thames and Hudson, London: 1990

Pidgeon Audio-Visual, PAV 796   'Nicholas Grimshaw – Industrial Architecture', 1979

Product & Process   Nicholas Grimshaw & Partners, London: 1988 (reprinted 1990)

RIBA Journal   June 1968: 'Buckminster Fuller: Royal Gold Medallist, 1968', Nick Grimshaw

RIBA Journal   October 1974: 'Survival by Design'

RIBA Journal   May 1976: 'Buildings as a Resource – Grimshaw on New Industrial Buildings'
RIBA Journal   October 1978: 'Timber Frame Infill Housing'
RIBA Journal   October 1980: 'Energetic Architecture', Nick Grimshaw
RIBA Journal   November 1983: 'British Architects Now'
RIBA Journal   January 1985: 'Grimshaw on New Industrial Buildings'
RIBA Journal   January 1994: 'Vanity Fare', Amanda Baillieu
RIBA Journal   March 1995: 'Our Man in Berlin'
RSA   18 January 1993: 'Better Buildings Mean Better Business', Report of a Symposium
Structural Steel Institute   1988: 'Corrosion Resistance'
Structure, Space and Skin: The Work of Nicholas Grimshaw & Partners   Rowan Moore (ed), Phaidon, London: 1993
Sunday Times   15 September 1991: 'Time for a High-Tech High-Flyer', Hugh Pearman
The State of British Architecture   Sutherland Lyall, The Architectural Press: 1980
The Times   10 November 1971: 'Partners in Design'
The Times   2 October 1991: 'Master whose Mettle is Galvanising', Marcus Binney
World Architecture   No 14, October 1991: 'White Knight of Technology', Martin Pawley
World Architecture – Special Report   March 1994: 'World Survey of Top 100 Architectural Practices'
World Architecture   No 23, April 1993: 'The Steady Ascent of Nicholas Grimshaw', Martin Pawley, 'Through Function to Beauty', Hugh Pearman, and Projects
World Architecture   No 25, August 1993: 'Great Coincidences', Guarino Guraini (Structure, Space and Skin)
World Architecture   No 29, May 1994: 'Technocracy: The Day of the Engineer', Paul Jodard

Service Tower, Student Hostel, London
Architects' Journal   1 May 1968: 'International Student Club', London
Architectural Design   October 1968: 'Conversion: The Farrell/Grimshaw Partnership's bathroom tower'
The Architectural Forum   July/August 1966, Preview: 'Plumbing as architecture'
Arkitekten   No 18, 1966: 'Clip-Kit'
Bauen und Wohnen   December 1967: 'Badezimmerturm aus Stahl und Kunststaff in Paddington'
Industrialised Building   September 1967: 'Steel and plastics bathroom tower'
Industrialised Building Systems & Components   February 1968
Journal of the British Constructional Steelwork Association Ltd   November 1967: 'A Tower Full of Baths'
Ove Arup & Partners Newsletter   February 1968: 'A Tower of Plastic Bathrooms', J N Martin
Structural Steel Design Awards   November 1969: British Steel Corporation
What's New In Building   September 1979: 'Plastics in Building'

Apartments, 125 Park Road, London
Architectural Design   October 1970: '125 Park Road'
Architectural Design   February 1973: 'Farrell/Grimshaw: Recent Work'
Architecture Intérieure Créé   May/June 1972: '125 Park Road'
Building Design   10 August 1970: 'The High-Rise High-Flyer', S Campbell
Express & News   18 December 1970: 'Park Road Newcomer', Christopher Sotch
Homes and Gardens   July 1972: 'The Same But Different', Christine Coleman
Observer Magazine   19 January 1975: 'More Space, Less Rooms', Margaret Duckett
RIBA Journal   October 1974: 'Survival by Design'
Sunday Mirror   18 April 1971: 'Success Storeys', Elizabeth Williamson & Shirley Lowe

Citroën Warehouse, Runnymede
Architectural Design   February 1973: 'Farrell/Grimshaw: Recent Work'
Building Dossier   22 February 1974: 'Warehouse at Runnymede, Surrey, England', Anthony Williams & Burles
Design   October 1972: 'Farrell-Grimshaw on Spec', Alistair Best
Financial Times   5 June 1974, José Manser
RIBA Journal   October 1974: 'Survival by Design'

Headquarters for Editions Van de Velde, Tours, France
Architects' Journal   April 1975: 'Editions Van de Velde, Bureau et Stockage'
Architecture Intérieure Créé   November/December 1979: 'Une Flexibilité bien tempérée'

Factory for Herman Miller, Bath
Architects' Journal   1 March 1978: 'Herman Miller Factory at Bath'
Architecture Intérieure Crée   February/March 1981: 'Grimshaw & Partners – de Bath à Nottingham'
Baumeister   October 1978: 'Möbelfabrik in Bath'
British Steel Corporation   October 1978: 'Framed in Steel 1'
Building   2 December 1977: 'Steely Spans'
Building   30 September 1983: 'Engineered for Elegance', Sutherland Lyall
Building Design   June 1977: Schemes shortlisted for FT Industrial Architecture Award
Daily Telegraph   18 July 1978: 'Futuristic factory can put on a new face', John Grigsby
Domus   November 1977: 'Miller on Avon'
Estates Times   11 November 1977: 'Design for Industry', Michael Foster
Herman Miller Inc   1978: 'A Statement of Expectations', Max de Pree
L'Industria delle Costruzioni   June 1979: 'Edificio Industriale sulle rive dell'Avon'
Observer   22 June 1980: 'The Flexible Factory', Stephen Gardiner
Progressive Architecture   July 1978: 'Trim-Tech', Barbara Goldstein
RIBA Journal   September 1977: 'Action Factory'
The State of British Architecture   Sutherland Lyall, The Architectural Press: 1980

Advanced Factory Units, Winwick Quay, Warrington
Baumeister   June 1980: 'Gewerbe und Kleinindustrie,
Vorrats–Industriehallen'
Building   9 March 1979: 'Zip-up Shed', Brian Waters
Building Dossier   28 October 1983: 'Winwick Quay',
Anthony Williams
Domus   June 1980: 'Flexible for Industry'
Progressive Architecture   August 1980: 'English Winners',
Penny McGuire
RIBA Journal   January 1980: 'Design for Change', Peter Murray
The State of British Architecture   Sutherland Lyall,
The Architectural Press: 1980

Headquarters for BMW , Bracknell
Architecture Contemporaine   1982/83, Anthony Krafft
Baumeister   April 1983: 'Herman Miller in Holland'
British Steel Corporation   October 1980: 'Framed in Steel 1'
Building   7 December 1984: 'Nerve of Steel', Sutherland Lyall
Deutsche Bauzeitung   October 1982: 'BMW in England', Eric Watson
L'Architecture d'aujourd'hui   15 December 1980: 'Verre et Acier –
High Tech Architecture?'
Progressive Architecture   August 1980: 'English Winners',
Penny McGuire
What's New In Building   March 1980: 'BMW Distribution
Centre, Bracknell'

Factory Units, Queen's Drive, Nottingham
Architecture Intérieure Créé   February/March 1981: 'Grimshaw &
Partners – de Bath à Nottingham'
Architectural Review   December 1980: 'Notts Domes: Factory, Castle
Park, Nottingham', Peter Davey
Baumeister   April 1983: 'Castle Park in Nottingham'
Chartered Surveyor Weekly   2 December 1982: 'Developing
Designs', Michael Hanson
L'Architecture d'aujourd'hui   15 December 1980: 'Verre et Acier –
High Tech Architecture?'
RIBA Journal   March 1981: 'Anthology of British Architecture'
RIBA Journal   April 1979, 'Four Examples of Advance Industrial
Buildings by Farrell/Grimshaw Partnership'

Sports Hall for IBM, Winchester
Architectural Review   March 1982: 'High-Tech Gym', John Winter
L'Architecture d'aujourd'hui   February 1985: 'Le High Tech n'est-il
qu'un style?'
L'Industria delle Costruzioni   March 1983: 'Centro Sportivo a
Winchester', Fliamma Dinelli
Space Design   No 244, January 1985: 'Nicholas Grimshaw & Partners'

Furniture Factory for Vitra, Weil-am-Rhein, Germany
Architectural Review   July 1983: 'Furniture Factory, Weil-am-Rhein,
West Germany'
Deutsche Bauzeitung   December 1983: 'Schnelle Kiste', Gunter Schnel
Domus   No 641, 1983: 'Ingredienti dell Nouvelle Usine'
L'Architecture d'aujourd'hui   September 1983: 'Usine et
Bureaux Vitra'
Space Design   No 244, January 1985: 'Nicholas Grimshaw & Partners'

Wiltshire Radio Station, Wootton Bassett
Building   5 August 1983: 'High-Tech Tune-In', Sutherland Lyall
Building Design   22 April 1983: 'Grimshaw Scores a Double Top',
Ted Stevens

Herman Miller Distribution Centre, Chippenham
Architects' Journal   4 September 1985: 'Construction Studies
High-Tech Cladding', Derek Osbourn
Architecture Contemporaine   1984/85, Anthony Krafft
Architecture Intérieure Créé   October/November 1985
Architecture Thématique: Usines   Electa-Monteur, 1987,
Jacques Ferrier
Architecture Today   Charles Jencks, Academy Editions, London: 1982
Architecture & Urbanism   September 1986: 'Nicholas Grimshaw
& Partners'
Architectural Design   British Architecture Profile, 1984
Building   30 September 1983: 'Engineered for Elegance',
Sutherland Lyall

Building Design   22 April 1983: 'Grimshaw Scores a Double Top',
Ted Stevens
RIBA Journal   September 1983: 'Herman Miller at Chippenham',
Peter Murray
RIBA Journal   November 1983: 'British Architecture Now'
Werke, Bauen und Wohnen   11 November 1984: 'Halle und Detail'

Ice Rink, Oxford
Architectural Review   March 1985: 'Oxford Schooner', Colin Davies
Building Dossier   12 April 1985: 'Oxford Ice Rink', Anthony Williams
& Partners
RIBA – Transactions 8   1986: 'Oxford Ice Rink', Nick Grimshaw
The Times on Saturday   7–13 April 1984: 'Skating into a New Ice
Age', Peter Waymark

Headquarters for Ladkarn, London Docklands
Architecture Intérieure Créé   October/November 1985: 'Tradition
High-Tech – Ladkarn Haulage'
Architecture & Urbanism   September 1986: 'Nicholas Grimshaw
& Partners'
Archithese   March 1988: 'Ladkarn Haulage Headquarters',
Steven Groak
Building   10 January 1986: 'Docklands Masterpiece – Rough
Diamond', Sutherland Lyall
Building   4 March 1988: 'Re-zipping a Shed', Martin Spring
Tubular Structures   No 41, February 1987: 'On the Waterfront'

Research Centre for Rank Xerox, Welwyn Garden City
AJ Focus   September 1989: Case Study, 'Blind Science'
Architects' Journal   July 1988: Focus, Product Review, Cladding
Architecture Today   September 1989: 'Between Function and Rhetoric', Richard Saxon
Arup Journal   Autumn 1989: 'Rank Xerox, Welwyn Garden City', Ian Gardner and Roger Johns
Building Design   8 April 1988: Products in Practice, 'Polymeric Roofing'
Building Services, The CIBSE Journal   March 1990: 'Top Ranking Services'
Detail   June 1990: Research and Development Centre, Welwyn Garden City
Insight   October 1987: Rank Xerox employees' magazine, Special Supplement
Logic Report   Spring 1990: 'The Flexible Office According to Rank Xerox'
RIBA Directory   January 1991: Award Winning Buildings: Industrial
RIBA Journal   January 1991: Regional Awards, Eastern
TBL Update   Summer 1991: 'Solar Shading for Rank Xerox'

Leisure Centre, Stockbridge
AJ Focus   June 1991: 'Waves Below the Mast'
Architecture Today   June 1991: 'Grimshaw's Stockbridge: Structure as Symbol', Robin Spence

Superstore for Sainsbury's, Camden, London
Architects' Journal   6 August 1986: 'Superstore Solutions'
Architects' Journal   4 October 1989: 'Market Leader', Stephen Gardiner, Martin Pawley and John Pringle
AJ Focus   March 1989: 'Checkout Fire Protection', Helen Heard
Architectural Record   September 1989: 'Heroic Transformations', Deborah K Dietsch
Architectural Review   October 1989: 'Urban Grimshaw'
Architecture Intérieure Créé   October/November 1989: 'Supermarche', Peter Davey
Architektur   September 1994: 'Architektur Am Wasser, London', Peter Clauhs
The Associate   October 1988: 'Three Modern Architects: All Work and No Play', Jon Stock
Atrium   March 1989: 'Talking to the Terrier', Neil Parkyn
Bauwelt   5 October 1990: 'Graue Fregatte, Silbener Rumpf'
Building Design   8 August 1986: 'Chain Reaction'
Building Design   3 February 1989: 'Structural Superstore', Sutherland Lyall
Detail   Issue 4, 1990: 'Housing and Supermarket in Camden Town, London'
Developments in Structural Engineering   21–23 August 1990, Proceedings of the Forth Rail Bridge Centenary Conference, 'J Sainsbury plc Supermarket at Camden', R E Slade
L'Arca   December 1990: 'Camden Tower', Jacopo della Fontana
L'Architecture d'aujourd'hui   February 1990: 'Le Goût de l'Ingénierie'
New Civil Engineer   12 May 1988: 'Sainsbury's Skeleton', Huw Jones
Observer   18 December 1988: 'Super Shed', Stephen Gardiner
Royal Fine Art Commission   Annual Report 1986
Style & Travel   26 December 1993: 'Check These Out', Hugh Pearman
Daily Telegraph   27 December 1988: 'Shape of Shops to Come', Kenneth Powell
Financial Times   23 December 1988: 'Setting Store in a Nautical Design', Gillian Darley
Guardian   12 December 1988: 'The Chain Store Massacre', Martin Pawley
Independent   24 March 1988: 'New Consumer Durables', Janet Abrams
RIBA   London Region Retail Supplement, 1987: 'Sainsbury Superstore', Martin Spring
RIBA Journal   November 1988: Director General's Column
RIBA Journal   September 1994: 'Courting Trouble', Louise Rogers
Sunday Times   11 December 1988: 'Checking out Modernism', Hugh Pearman
Time Out   4 January 1989: 'Store Wars', Joanne Glasbey & Pol Ferguson-Thompson

Houses at Grand Union Walk, Camden, London
Blueprint   September 1989: 'On a Wing and a Prayer'
Daily Telegraph   16 August 1989: 'Plunder on the Retail Waterfront', Dixie Nichols
Guardian   11 July 1989: 'Best of British', Martin Pawley
Sunday Telegraph   4 November 1990: 'Modern Marvels', Anoop Parikh
Sunday Times   29 October 1989: 'To Boldly Live', Hugh Pearman
Techniques & Architecture   June/July 1990: 'Masque et Marque'
Time Out   7–14 March 1990: 'Home Truths', Jan Burney

Homebase Store, Brentford
Architects' Journal   29 June 1988: 'Warehouse on the Wing', John Winter
The British Constructional Steelwork Association Ltd   1988/89, Annual Report
Building   15 January 1988. 'Masted Craftsman', Graham Ridout
Detail   May/June 1988: 'Superstore in Brentford'
Taywood News   Christmas 1987: 'Myton – The Heavy Lift'
Techniques & Architecture   August/September 1988: 'Entrepot: La métaphore d'un biplan Magasin Homebase près de l'aéroport d'Heathrow'
The Structural Engineer   19 April 1988: 'Cover Story'

Financial Times Printing Works, London Docklands

AJ Focus   October 1988: 'Maximum Vision', Mike Stacey

AJ Focus   July 1991: 'Shaping Up,' Insight: Frank Holliday

AMC Revue d'Architecture   June 1988: 'Verre colle aux Docks de Londres'

Archi-Crée   December 1989/January 1990: 'Murs de Verre et Tourelles d'Acier'

Architect, Builder, Contractor and Developer   June 1989: Exterior Cladding, 'Heroic Facade'

Architects' Journal   9 June 1993: 'Marine Technology Transfer', John Rowson

Architects' Journal   July 1988: Focus, Product Review

Architects' Journal   26 July 1989: Letters, 'Practice and Preaching', Julian Boswell

Architects' Journal   6 December 1989: 'News' re Civic Trust Awards

Architects' Journal   20 and 27 December 1989: Review of the Decade, 'Muddling Through', Robert Cowan

Architects' Journal   25 July 1990: BBC Design Awards

Architects' Journal   May 1991: Book Review: 'Financial Times Print Works: Nicholas Grimshaw & Partners', by David Jenkins. Review by Stephen Greenberg

Architectural Record   September 1989: 'Heroic Transformations', Deborah K Dietsch

Architectural Review   November 1988: 'Glass Wall in Blackwall, John Winter

Architectural Review   April 1989: Criticism, 'Housing, Isle of Dogs and Bermondsey, London Docklands', Frances Anderton, and Products Survey

Architecture in Detail   Financial Times Printing Works, David Jenkins, Phaidon Press, London: 1991

Architecture Today   July 1990: 'Steel and 92', Bob Latter

Baumeister   July 1989: 'Zeitungsdruckerei in London'

Blueprint   November 1988: 'A Sign of the Times', Hugh Aldersey-Williams

Blueprint   June 1989: Briefing, 'Why put Design in a Museum?', exhibition review by Charlotte Ellis

Bovis Review   June 1988: 'Display of Excellence'

Building   15 April 1988: Technology Special – Piling and Foundations, 'Underlying Principles', Dr Ken Fleming

Building   21 July 1989: 'Conder in acquisitive mood as reorganisation pays off', Peter Cooper

Building   12 October 1990: 'Evidence for the Prosecution: Traditional Method. Financial Times Printworks', Neil Parkyn

Building Design   Supplement, March 1989: 'Nocturnal Habitation'

Building Design   1 December 1989, Civic Trust Awards

Building Design   Supplement, March 1988: 'Hi-tech Docklands Look in the Pink'

Building Design   16 December 1988: 'Buildings of the Year'

Building Design   15 September 1989: 'Truro Court and FT Tie for Prize'

Building Products   March 1990: BAL Fact File No 11, 'Financial Times Building'

Business   November 1988: 'Press Revelation', Jonathan Glancey

Civic Trust Awards   November 1989: Introduction and 'Award – Tower Hamlets'

De Architect Thema   May 1989: 'Krantendrukkerij Financial Times, London'

Design Week   26 May 1989: 'Docklands Design is Put in the Dock', Sutherland Lyall

Design Week   26 June 1990: 'Day of Reckoning for the BBC First Fifteen'

Deutsche Bauzeitschrift   March 1990: 'Financial Times Druckerei gebäude in London'

Evening Standard   12 December 1989: 'Watts On...', Ian Irvine

Financial Times   28 March 1989: 'Goodbye Bracken House, Hello Southwark Bridge', Colin Amery

Financial Times   5 September 1988: 'Move to Docklands Printing', Raymond Snoddy

Financial Times   26 October 1988: 'PM opens FT Print Plant', 'A letter to FT readers from the Editor', Geoffrey Owen

Financial Times   22 January 1990: 'Buildings Speak Louder than Words', Colin Amery

Illustrated London News   Winter 1989: '1989 London Awards'

Independent   29 May 1989: 'Glazed Expression', Mark Swenarton

Independent   5 July 1989: 'Architecture Awards for Prince's Critic', Ian Mackinnon

L'Arca   October 1990: 'La nuova sede del Financial Times' (The New Financial Times Head Office), Luigi Moiraghi

L'Architecture d'aujourd'hui   February 1990: 'Imprimérie du Financial Times à Londres'

London Dockland Architectural Review   1989: 'Financial Times Printing Works'

The Monotype Recorder   1988: 'The FT – A Blueprint for New Design'

New Builder   26 October 1989: British Construction Industry Awards 1989

New Builder   9 November 1989: 'Right Pace for Printing Works', letter

New Civil Engineer   26 October 1989: 'Inner Vision', Jacqui Robbins

New Civil Engineer   1 December 1988: 'Cover Story – Drama on a Tight String', David Fowler

Newspaper Focus   February 1990: 'The Glass Mirage', Pat Briscoe

Perspective   1988: 3rd quarter, Financial Times Group, 'Lift-off at East India Dock'

Progressive Architecture   December 1988: 'Selected Details'

RIBA Journal   January 1990: 'RIBA Awards for Architecture'

RIBA Journal   July 1988: re cladding

RIBA Journal   July 1989: Cladding and Glazing Update

RIBA Journal   August 1989: Awards for the Region

Sunday Times   10 September 1989: 'Good, Better, Best', Hugh Pearman

Sunday Times   2 July 1989: 'The New Fleet Street', Hugh Pearman

The Times   29 October 1989: 'Palaces with a Practical Purpose'

Werke, Bauen und Wohnen   July 1994: 'Ein Glaspalast fur der Altag', Petra Hagen Hodgson

Wohn Design   January/February 1995: 'Welcome to London – Architecture and Design', Ingrid Nowel

Nicholas Grimshaw & Partners
The Team 1965–88

(people who worked in the NPG office
during the period of the projects in this book)

Simon Allford
Simon Bean
Mark Bryden
Christopher Campbell
Jim Dorsett
Sally Draper
Laura Evans
Mark Fisher
Rowena Fuller
Zully Garcia
Paul Gibson
Mark Goldstein
David Grawford
Don Gray
Paul Grayshon
Nick Grimshaw
David Harriss
David Heeley
Christine Humphreys
Guiseppe Intini
Kevin Jackson
Eva Jiricna
Matthew Keeler
Douglas Keys
David Kirkland

Rosie Latter
Frank Ling
Ian McArdle
Philip McLean
Roger Meadows
Christopher Nash
David Nixon
William O'Brien
Norman Partridge
John Prevc
David Richmond
Graham Saunders
Gunther Schnell
Jeff Scherer
Ulrike Seifritz
Neven Sidor
Janina Szymbra
Brian Taggart
Hin Tan
Simon Templeton
Mark Walker
Gill Wallace
Andrew Whalley
Trisha Williams
Wolfgang Zimmer